Me Paradox

Gain the Social Business Edge

Over 50 Online Reputation Management Guidelines to Differentiate Your Career

Chae J. Pak

New World
Tustin, California

Me Paradox: Gain the Social Business Edge
Over 50 Online Reputation Management Guidelines to Differentiate Your Career
Copyright © 2010 by Chae J. Pak

Published by New World
Tustin, California

Printed in the United States of America
Library of Congress LCCN: 2010917266

ISBN-10 0-615-42161-X
ISBN-13 9780615421612

The following trademarks are the property of their respective owners: AdWeek, Alexa, Amazon, American Chemical Society, American Medical Association, Apple and iTunes, Archive.org, aSmallWorld, Bebo, Blockbuster, Blogpulse, Chicago Bulls, Christian Science Monitor, CIO, Cisco, CNN, Compete.com, Craigslist, Daypop, De.licio.us, Designerid, Digg, eBay, eHow, eLance, EMC, Facebook, Flickr, Friendster, Fox News, General Electric, Gizmodo, GoDaddy, Google, GraphicDefine.org, Harry Potter, Huffington Post, IBM, Intel, Jive Software, K12, Last Night Shots, LinkedIN, Lufthansa, Mechdir.com, Meetup.com, Microsoft, MySpace, NASA, Netflix, NY Times, New York Stock Exchange, Nike, Ning, oDesk, Oracle, Pipl.com, Plaxo, Plentyoffish.com, Red Sox, ReputationDefender.com, Salesforce, SAP, Scriptlance, Slashdot, SolidWorks, Squidoo, Technorati, Tosback.org, Trackur.com, Twitter, Urlfan.com, VM Ware, vWorker, Wal-mart, Weather Channel, Web MD, Wired, Wikipedia, Word of Mouth, Yahoo!, Yelp, Zabasearch, and ZoomInfo.

To my wife Rosshalde for all her support and patience

Table of Contents

chapter four

chapter five

chapter six

chapter seven

~introduction~
Change Perspective, Change Your Life

Many of us are disengaged from our jobs. We go to work so that we can pay our bills or get away from the house. Somewhere between starting high school and starting a family, we forgot who we were and what we were passionate about.

Why is it that when we are children we are told to dream, explore, and become whatever made us happy? And then the day came when it all changed. Pursuing such aspirations was seen as impractical and out of question–irrational even. Does being an adult mean that we have to leave behind what captivated us as a child?

For many of us, we cannot just simply change our career paths, however, we can change our disposition, if empowered. Unifying who you truly are and who you have to be at work is possible, but it is not trivial. *Me Paradox* was written for those who desire to be driven by passion rather than necessity; to do better, to get involved, interact, share and give freely. Yes, the volatile future is filled with risk, yet risk needs to be viewed as a prerequisite to gain, not something to be feared and avoided.

It's a different era. Now is your opportunity to do more than succeed, to rediscover your passion and rouse your heart to be in tune with what you do and how you do it. The Me Paradox is more than an ordinary business activity. It is a way to find deeper meaning, something that touches the soul with timeless attributes like love, honor, truth, justice, and beauty.

What is the Me Paradox? To make this less of an abstraction, let's start with a paradox in general.

We are all familiar with one or more types of paradoxes, like which came first the chicken or the egg. Or, to understand the future one must look to the past. Paradoxes defy reason, what we consider logical and what should have happened according to what we know and understand. Another paradox that comes to mind is what economists call the "productivity paradox." It attempts to explain why the rapid advances in technology are met with the relatively slow growth of productivity.

Merriam-Webster defines "paradox" as a statement that is seemingly contradictory but is perhaps true. Paradoxes exist to help us reconcile events, concepts, truths, we believe are so but can't explain. For instance, if technology does not improve worker productivity, then why do businesses increasingly spend more money and human resources on it?

The advent of the Internet and social technologies has created another such paradox. We see it in the billions of people who use and participate in it. Intuitively, we are all doing things that make sense but we cannot determine what this superhighway of information and connections is exactly, and how best to use it to our advantage.

Many have tried to capture it, analyze, and frame it for the world to understand. This book, although along that same pursuit, takes a different stance. Rather than claiming the discovery of some universal truth, this book aims to understand the causes of it, and explore the few known concepts and tactics to navigate it. The rest remains, as most paradoxes do, a gut feeling, something that defies logic.

The Me Paradox, within the context of the social web, is not about leisure or games, but a profound shift in how we manage ourselves. We are no longer just about our own relative experiences and built-in personalities, but a similar composite of other people connected to us. This gives way to the paradox of me, where the key is to stop focusing only on yourself and, instead, put your efforts into bettering other people. The paradox here is that, when you follow this protocol and gain access to the collective, the better informed and resource rich you are. It also brings you closer to peers, colleagues, and customers–to the cusp of innovation. Axiomatically, you get what you put into people. That is the Me Paradox.

It is important to remain outwardly focused as you read this book. The way you interpret and comprehend the material should be from a holistic perspective. Investigate those around you, and reflect to get a better sense of who you are. You may believe what you know and how you act is all your own, but when you finish this book and go out and live the Me Paradox, you will realize that even your own intimate, very private view of the world, is a mere reflection of the people around you–even those who you do not know yet.

~chapter one~

Brave New Technological World

You've heard the hype. Technology is changing the world so you better get onboard. But every where you look, it's information overload. What should you pay attention to in this vast sea of technological advances?

In some arenas, we have learned from experience or the mistakes of others, so we know better than to make the same mistakes again. Some of us rode the roller-coaster of the dotcom era, and now we're avoiding the excesses. We've handled the massive changes wrought by the Internet. We're older, wiser, and prepared to meet any challenges these new technologies could pose as they enter our workplace.

Or, are we?

It seems every time we think we have a handle on things, they change. This time around it's **Web 2.0**, Social Media, Social Networking. Every era has their different products, but the story remains the same: on the scene bursts a dazzling, disruptive technology; the younger generation flocks to it, absorbing it into their DNA, and then along come the adults, reluctant but eventually accepting. Finally, it makes its way into business. And somehow, overnight, it becomes indispensable. Email. Internet. IM chat. Amazing, transformative tools. They have changed the way you find and do your job today.

If you're old enough to remember the early days of web browsers, you're likely among the next wave of business leaders. To the generation just entering the workforce, using Social Media is like breathing air. These twenty-somethings know the technology, but are generally limited to a couple of years of work experience. Those of us who have been on the job for decades can feel threatened by the younger generation's savvy use of technology. But, with the right tools and right attitude, anyone can prosper.

And, attitude does matter.

It is hard to deny that those who prefer to stay stuck in traditional thought-patterns are going to be behind the curve.

Today and tomorrow, the business world will be led by the 30- to 55-year-olds. In this group, emerging technologies are largely new and alien. And if you are a member of this group and think your Facebook or LinkedIN account is adequate preparation for business and networking, think again.

Adopting New Technology—It's Worth It

What if the hype is for real? That this new social technology is not simply a tool. That it won't just change the way you do your job today, but it will change how you manage your career, the way you relate to your co-workers and to people in general. It will change the way you think. That is, if you can adapt.

The current generation of leaders is about to face the challenge of their lifetime, and it's not 'The Recession'. This challenge goes to the heart of corporate culture, business processes, and organizational practices, and it's a challenge for which most of us are not even remotely prepared. There are no historical precedents. Nothing could have prepared us for the technological changes that lie ahead.

But just because the changes are unprecedented does not mean you should take a fatalistic approach. The adaptive approach is healthier. And, there are steps that you can take to prepare yourself and your business to stay in pace with technological advances. This book will outline these steps in detail in later chapters, but first read about how embracing a new culture and adapting to new technologies worked out well for one NASA employee.

Saving the Dream through Radical Ingenuity

When Nicholas Skytland was just a kid he dreamt of working for NASA, an organization that produced some of mankind's greatest achievements. He spent almost an entire lifetime preparing for the competitive hiring process. Then, at age 27, once his dreams had come to fruition, he was haunted by a thought. What if everything he had worked so hard for went up in smoke? He knew NASA had an intractable public relations problem. And he now had research in his hands showing the future was far worse than anyone realized.

Thirty years ago, NASA was the symbol of American ingenuity, bravery, and innovation. Years later, it was widely perceived as a reactionary throwback, outmoded, stuck in its ways, a symbol of Cold War command-and-control mentality. It had never fully recovered from the black eye of the Challenger and Columbia disasters, and despite subsequent successes like the Mars mission, it seemed outdated, behind the times, and increasingly irrelevant. With the federal budget facing the competing priorities of global warming, wars, poverty, and crumbling infrastructure, the tremendous sums NASA demanded for space exploration seemed, if anything, irresponsible.

Skytland thought: What if the institution he loved since childhood and spent a lifetime preparing for was unable to change its image?

Skytland, in his EVA Physiology Systems and Performance Project had done his homework and knew the American demographic was changing. As part of this performance project within the Human Adaptation and Countermeasures Division of the Space Life Science Directorate, Skytland had read the in-house reports and learned a few things about the generation he belonged to. This generation, made of up 70 million people, was currently 25% of the workforce. By 2014 the number would reach 47%. That meant that half of the workforce would come from **Generation Y**. Even more worrisome, 50% of his generation, the one that would be asked to pay the majority of the tax bill for NASA's budget, was either not aware of or not engaged in NASA's mission. A full 40% opposed it outright. 39% thought nothing worthwhile had ever come out of NASA.[1]

The future of NASA seemed bleak unless it could connect to Nicholas Skytland's generation, engage, and involve them in its mission. This went beyond public relations. NASA would have to transform its culture in order to survive.

To Skytland, the solution seemed obvious. NASA, Skytland will tell you, is a great place to work, full of brilliant, motivated people, but the culture just wasn't keeping up with the times. The idea was brilliant: get these facts in front of people, sort of introduce management to the ones footing the bill in an engaging way, but also start the grassroots effort of changing the organization. In February 2008, he joined forces with other twenty-somethings at NASA and formed OpenNasa.com. Skytland and Garret Fitzpatrick, in an impromptu task, used social media to connect the incredible Intellectual Capital at NASA, then to connect NASA to the world, the younger generation in particular.

Skytland and Fitzpatrick, with their sophisticated understanding of organizational change, were able to show the higher ups at NASA that it takes both ground-up and top-down efforts. They made sure management knew that NASA needed to begin reaching out with these technologies now, both in and out of the organization. In four short months, what they were able to achieve was nothing short of astounding:

- Presented their ideas to several management teams
- Created the Leadership forum
- Developed Co-op Advanced Planning Team (CAPT)
- Facilitated the JSC PAO New Media Project with CAPT
- Co-op Alumni Mentoring
- Established connections at Rice University
- Collaborated with Wired Magazine on Article Concept
- Led the planning of Yuri's Night Houston 08
- Created the Flat NASA Experiment Blog
- Used Facebook to inspire the public regarding NASA careers
- Connected NASA to Twitter
- Outreach. Lots of outreach

Their success created a stir within NASA and they generated responses. While their efforts are ongoing, they helped the organization set its sights on the right goal: recruiting and winning the hearts of the next generation.

Keep in mind, these things don't happen overnight. Internally, the pace of change is slower with this type of grass-roots effort. The pace might even lead one to believe that wide-scale change within large organizations is still far off. But, don't be fooled by appearances. In businesses and organizations throughout the modern world, a more radical transformation is already underway, and will be in full effect far sooner than most of us expect.

The Needs of the Enterprise

Chief information officers cite two main issues as the most important problems facing them: 1) How to deal with the aging workforce, capture their knowledge and expertise before they leave, and 2) how to support the incoming generation, this new breed of technically-savvy college grads, the **Millennials** or Generation Y, whose culture is increasingly at odds with the enterprise.

In other words (and this is for the older generation of business men and women), the company is looking for ways to capture your knowledge and render you replaceable by lower-priced, faster-learning, more technologically-savvy knowledge workers.

This might sound discouraging, but don't despair. Although it's not a far-fetched cost-cutting measure, there are ways to overcome it.

Social media is a good place to begin. Workers who can use and leverage these tools actually perform better at their jobs than those who don't. It's not necessarily what you know, but how fast you can find what you're looking for, and the quality of people you consult to help you make decisions.

The numbers tell the story. A 2007 McKinsey study[2] demonstrated that high-performing employees have networks 1/3 larger than the average. They leverage their networks for both information-sharing and decision-making. These same high performers account for a disproportionate amount of productivity compared to their peers: 40% more in operations, 49% in management, and 67% in sales. Other research[3] suggests the frequency of the information that employees take action on that comes from people in their network has more than doubled since 2006. Companies are aware of these changes and they are taking action. Kaiser Permanente, John Deere, EMC, Cisco, and Bank of America are just some of the Fortune 500 companies who are ahead of the game when it comes to their knowledge of today's employee and their networking strategies.

Much of the software these employees use has been here all along. First came social media tools for your business like wikis, blogs, and instant messaging that you've come to recognize. More recently, with the ascent of Facebook and LinkedIN, and then Twitter, people saw the value of making connections and forming networks. Starting in 2006, people began putting these pieces together to create a new breed of networking tool–Social Business Software. You'll note that the critical ingredient in this blend is the Social aspect, the ability to find and connect with people in order to work better.

If this is new to you, this book will explain each of these things in depth, show you the ways in which your particular workplace is going to change, and provide you with the practical steps you will need in order to survive when the business world is turned on its head.

If you are already a tech-savvy individual entering the business world, it will help you stay on top of your game so you don't fall behind as technology continues to advance.

Let's be realistic. The latest technological tools will always put older generations at a distinct disadvantage. But those with decades of experience who take the time to learn and use advancing technologies are indispensable. The question then is: What are you willing to do to compete on this newly-leveled playing field? Do you want to continue playing ball or retreat to the bench? The choice is up to you.

"Radical" is the New "Innovative"

Changes in technology are more drastic than people realize. The way they're entering your workplace is unassuming enough. If the notion of a "Facebook for the Enterprise" application sounds like a way for employees to waste time, then consider this: Innovative companies like Intel, Apple, and VM Ware realize that the people who matter, the leaders and most productive workers, will not waste any more time in a social network application than they do on the web, email, or instant message.

These corporate gurus are ahead of the curve in making themselves aware of the business models like **Network Effects** and **Long Tail**.

They also have examined how new strategies can be cultivated to foster productivity, creativity, and innovation, as well as speed time to market. They know the tools are viral and will take root in the organization. If you haven't seen them yet in your organization, check again. They are entering in through the back door right now, and will soon be everywhere.

Risks abound, however, and the biggest risk of all is when professionals latch onto the traditional notions of business. By doing this, they squander opportunities to take their career to another level, and may find themselves in a struggle to remain competitive. At stake here is not just the fate or careers of a few individuals, or a class of individuals—it's an entire generation. If today's professionals don't "get with it" this issue will ultimately limit their potential growth and the greatest opportunity available in years to adapt and capture a leadership position in the **New Economy** will have been lost.

Today's tools are viral, and inherently intuitive. They are not much of a challenge to technically learn and use. The key to finding the proper way to use them, navigate them, and reap the full potential gains, however, is far from easy.

It involves a different way of thinking. Letting everyone know what your favorite hobbies are in your profile is easy; building an online reputation or network of reliable co-producers is something different altogether. The landscape is riddled with treasures and landmines. On one side: riches. On the other: career disaster. In the middle, in the land of no-decision, is job instability, doubt, and wasted time and resources.

It will take more than just learning a new skill set. A subtle, but powerful psychological shift is in order. *Me Paradox* captures the essence of this shift and, through online reputation management, gives you practical tools not just to survive, but to achieve gains you never thought possible.

It's all About Me–Or is It?

Recent media dialogue contrasting Generation Y with the rest of society, while sometimes illuminating, offers little in the way of practical guidance. Further it may do considerable harm, as framing the discussion this way seems to necessarily tie this set of qualities to a particular age group when in reality these are skills to be learned.

The Me Paradox is a phrase used throughout the book to refer to something not bound to any particular generation, job type or function, and industry. Any person can embody the Me Paradox mentality; anyone can make this psychological shift.

Despite all the changes we see around us, we are still in the very beginnings of this societal transformation. There are major gains to be made by:

- **Networking**–Radically increasing the number of people you come into contact with.
- **Collaboration**–Performing your work reflectively.
- **Transparency**–Thinking and acting in the open.
- **Social Capital**–Lifting controls on most kinds of information, and voluntarily giving up of many forms of knowledge.
- **Presence**–Reflection as a function of membership.

For the majority of the population, particularly in the business sector, the very idea sounds unrealistic. It involves doing things most people today would consider potentially reputation damaging, even taboo. But letting yourself go before your peers and superiors essentially means de-emphasizing the importance of Me, and putting more focus on and stock in the crowd. And the chief paradox is that the more we minimize the Me and become outwardly focused–by putting ourselves out there consulting with and relying on others–the stronger, the more connected, and the more successful the Me becomes.

Much is made of the narcissism in society, in our peers and the youth we see filling out extensive profiles in Facebook. What signal does this convey? We think, "they're so full of themselves!" But isn't it more narcissistic to believe you can work out all issues by yourself, think in a vacuum, work alone until, voila, you let your work be recognized by the world!

These newcomers to the business world are not being given enough credit for the extent that they have let go of personal ownership of work and thought to the point that they understand how to identify with the crowd. It is this ability, this willingness, and this openness to criticism that will be the top-line predictor of success in the New Economy. Not only will this create new opportunities to stand out and lead, this new set of tools will make it increasingly difficult for those who hoard knowledge, slack off, or try to fall under the radar. They provide a powerful set of measurements for managers and social network analysts who expose those who don't share their knowledge, or who try to blend into the shadows. Those who are not participating will be viewed as deadwood. They will be the first to be shed in layoffs and the last to find jobs.

Along those same lines, what about the belief that your skills alone will land you your next job; that your resume, out of the simple merits of your schooling and experiences, will bubble you up out of a sea of thousands also applying for the same position? To some new and contemporary companies, a paper resume is laughable. Just talk to 30-year career veterans about their struggle putting their resume into ZoomInfo or LinkedIN–what would you wager on the bet it was probably their grown child that made the transport and not them?

'An Attitude; not a Technology'

The term "Web 2.0" was coined in 1999 by Darcy DiNucci. In her article, *Fragmented Future*, DiNucci writes:

> The Web we know now [...] is only an embryo of the Web to come. The first glimmerings of Web 2.0 are beginning to appear, and [...] will be understood not as screenfulls of text and graphics but as a transport mechanism, the ether through which interactivity happens.

By this time, the industry had fallen into the bad habit of producing websites that were no more than static brochures and magazines in online form. This fell painfully short of the medium's immense possibilities. Innovative online applications like Del.icio.us, Google Maps, Digg, Amazon, eBay, and Flickr capitalize on this, captivating the imagination and wowing the public. Industry woke from its stupor and realized that people needed help understanding the developments, technologies, and user perspectives that made these websites unique. Web 2.0 sent the message that something new was happening, and forced the industry to figure out what that was. When companies met in 2002, their discussion led to the conference name Web 2.0 two years later. When they popularized the term, it was the right name at the right time. But Internet Alchemy's Ian Davis said it best when he further defined Web 2.0 as "an attitude, not a technology."

Today, the term Web 2.0 is falling out of vogue. Social media and its variants are on the rise and taking the place of Web 2.0 as measured by the most searched terms on the Internet. The message of Web 2.0 has been received. The stupendous success in the consumer space makes the message contained in Web 2.0 no longer necessary, but the attitude still remains.

These technologies have arrived at the business, and they are about to change your world. Where **Enterprise 2.0** has been the Web 2.0 corollary aimed at corporations, Social Business[4] is the evolution of Web 2.0, and it affects everyone in businesses, large, medium, or small. Moreover, this term puts the focus back on Social, and by extension the full range of change now in play: social, cultural, economic, and technological.

Age is not a Barrier

Despite the complicated nature of the technologies that exist behind the scenes, there's good news in all of this. The Me Paradox is available to anyone, regardless of age, skill, or background. The fact that you've noticed a psychological shift and are willing to learn the skills puts you ahead of the curve. At the very least, applying the material here will enable you to compete on even footing with anyone in the New Economy.

Changes seem to favor the younger generation, but this trend is temporary. Like it or not, new technology has always caught on with the young first. The intention is not to stir up generational antagonism or reverse the 60's dictum "Don't trust anyone over 30." Counter-examples of savvy 60-year-olds and Luddite teenagers abound. However it's important to remember that the advantage the young have is the ability to keep an open mind about changes, a skill that does not have to be restricted to youth alone. Rather than waiting for the youth to lead you, capitalize on these findings now to lead the youth, the demographic that will shortly make up half the workforce.

Business-as-Usual is the Wave of the Past

Me Paradox doesn't claim to have all the answers. But, what this book can do is give you the tools you will need to navigate and create your own brand in the fast growing world of the social web. These include skills, methods founded on best practices, and the experience-based guidance. It's human nature to want answers that are black and white, with no uncertainty. But the reality is that in the rapidly advancing world of technology, we are all trying to keep up.

Social business is at the center of those changes. Trying to go on doing business-as-usual puts us at risk of becoming obsolete, isolated relics unable to manage future prospects or achieve goals. On the other hand, we must be careful not to engage haphazardly. We have all heard about career-ending Facebook disasters. I realize there are others spreading a similar message; this book is the only one that combines the various messages to provide you with something actionable.

My approach comes from a confluence of sources that provide unique insights that need to be shared so that society can benefit from the experience of others. Each of those sources contains only a piece of the puzzle: Current academic research is focused on teenagers' use of social media, with findings demonstrating how their minds and social relationships have been changed as a result of the technology. Analyst organizations are working to keep up with the practical implications of this information. Thought leaders are collecting more anecdotal information to add nuance to the body of knowledge. And, the corporations who have embraced social media have great incentive to conduct research that bridges the gap from theory to dollars and cents. This constantly expanding body of knowledge can be overwhelming. My goal is to guide you, the business person, in the steps you will take as you navigate through this web of immense technology; *Me Paradox* will help you create an action plan.

This plan will also help make you more comfortable with the conflicting information that pervades the web, especially concerning social media: "Facebook is the new form of business networking!"

"You lose your privacy on Facebook and can embarrass yourself horribly!" There's a tendency to be thrown off balance by every new wave in this flood of information. We have to get our balance so we can ride the waves, acting strategically even as we cope with the multitude of changes. The good news is two-fold: the benefits outweigh the risks many times over, and anyone can learn to thrive within the social web.

It's true that the use of social media like Facebook is becoming much more pervasive even in a business setting. And, yes, it's also true that you can embarrass yourself horribly on Facebook–if you reveal too much. Once you learn how much is appropriate for your unique and personal situation, you will be prepared to use Facebook to your own best advantage. As you continue to gain confidence, you will take incremental steps that bring you closer and closer to the goals you want. Social media will be useful in a much larger sense than just staying in touch with friends; it will help you advance your career towards your ultimate goals.

Your Network: The Smartest Being You Know

The idea of focusing on others to develop one's own possibilities may seem contradictory, but this is not a new concept. Historically, the professional self has always been connected to professional networks. The marketplace was an antiquated form of modern technology. The book *Cluetrain Manifesto*[5] emphasizes that before most modern technology, the marketplace was not just a place to exchange goods, it was a place to exchange ideas, a place to get access to critical knowledge. Doing business was also a way to move around information. Even today, in order to obtain information, we need to connect with other people–people we trust. Technology lets us use social media to connect, and when we participate in these online exchanges, others need to trust us. That trust is built on reputation. That your reputation is the sum of people's image of you is not only an example of the Me Paradox, it's one of the keys to using the Me Paradox to your advantage.

Technology Evolves; We Evolve

In order to understand the nature of the Me Paradox, a little background is necessary. The emergence of new technologies has driven the evolution of social business through three major developmental phases: the Technology-Centric phase, the Content-Centric phase, and the People-Centric phase.

In the Technology-Centric phase, the first few tools began to emerge. They were BBSes and listservs with clunky interfaces, but they enabled tremendous strides in communication. Far-flung acquaintances could discuss matters instantly, and entire networks of people began to talk regularly about every topic under the sun. The technology was crude but it was new and that defined it. The first online social business pioneers were people who understood the technology and were willing to live with its limitations. Despite its limitations, it held promise for a world that would be more connected through technology. It was hard to imagine the refinement that would come later.

Then, around 1994, we saw the beginnings of the Content-Centric age. With this came Knowledge Management Systems, Content Management Systems, and the materialization of the World Wide Web. Technology's limitations were no longer its defining feature, and valuable information started to become available. The focus at the time was to create as much content as possible in this new medium. People started out-using the metaphors they were familiar with. Content repositories were organized in sets of file folders, with complicated hierarchies. Since then, entire careers have been devoted to Information Architecture and Design and Information Management.

With the onset of the People-Centric phase, social technologies began to overtake purely content-oriented technologies. More and more information is now available, and searching for that information is becoming easier as technology advances and more and more people participate: The connections or networks of people that recognize and leverage the individual contributions of the many versus the centralized production of a few is becoming more valuable. Many aspects of the technology have been around for some time, (think back to AOL or Friendster), but the refinement and understanding of the technology has changed. The creators of these applications finally reached the crucial point where a critical mass of users were able to understand it and reap its benefits.

As technology has evolved, it has changed from a paradigm where users access content, to an exciting online world where communities create and share ideas, and, this is where social networking comes into play. Facebook, which debuted in 2004, is one of the most popular websites in the World Wide Web. It now boasts a user base of 500 million, surpassing any other social network on the World Wide Web. At its core, Facebook is an interface for users to interact with one another. Users can chat, share photographs, or just let their "friends" know their current status. Twitter, which arrived in 2006, has used a simpler approach to social networking and it is currently one of the fastest growing websites on the Web. It limits its users to a small profile, status updates called "Tweets," and it even has character limits on those status updates so people don't get too wordy.

The Web is becoming less about content and more about individual social connections. Your personal knowledge potential has grown, and now includes the knowledge of anyone in your web of online contacts–on top of what's searchable. This participatory element means broad cultural changes are on the horizon. In this day and age, you have the power to change your destiny more than in any other time in history.

To use an analogy, thanks to social networking, grassroots movements now have the ability to move across several football fields in record time. No longer are they restricted to flyers, phone calls, and door-to-door operations: organizing can be done quickly and easily online, making voices echo across cities, communities, and the entire world. As you might expect, the business world is awake and paying attention to the developments.

RESEARCH SUMMARY

In 2005, Tim O'Reilly put the world on notice of the massive changes about to sweep the planet in his paper, *What is Web 2.0?* Speaking largely to thought leaders and technology executives, he identified the basic tenets of the new breed of Internet applications, and their associated economic, social, and technological implications. At the time of the conference, more than a billion people had Internet access, half of them broadband. Mobile devices outnumbered desktops by a factor of two. O'Reilly was among the first to ask what would become of the economy and society once people were massively connected at all times. These trends were growing at a remarkable rate, he said, and soon would be ubiquitous. Inevitably, the enterprise space, dubbed Enterprise 2.0, would follow suit.

Four years later, O'Reilly's predictions came to fruition. Today there are more than a billion users on the Internet,[6] 84 million using broadband in the US alone,[7] and GSMA reports[8] nearly three quarters of the world's population has a mobile device. The Web 2.0 breed of Internet applications has now reached the tipping point with 400 million Facebook users[9] and 184 million blogs.[10]

In 2008, Google alone made $20 billion dollars plus with 80% of the search market.[11] Social media was crowned champion of the Internet mindshare in 2009, and although it has not perfected the monetization of its business model, Michael Arrington of TechCrunch recently reported that a recommendation on a social networking site is 700% more effective than a recommendation presented on Google, making this technology giant very nervous and grabbing the attention of powerful people.

The numbers are eye-catching, but the degree that social media impacts the daily lives of its users is even more telling. In 2007, a Pew Internet and American Life Project survey[12] reported that 48 percent of all social network users visit their profile daily to catch up on the updates, messages, and media posted by members of their network. That combination of 26% who visit at least once a day and the 22% who visit more than once a day, make social networking a daily fixture for nearly fifty percent of all users' lives. Match that with continuing exponential growth in adoption noted above and we can foresee the extent of its eventual reach. In these public sites, 91% use social networking sites to keep up with friends, and around a third are already using it for non-personal reasons. The fact that 1 out of 18 people globally have a Facebook account shows that this is not a fad. It's a broad and far–reaching, culture-changing trend.

While adoption in the Enterprise lags the consumer space, as O'Reilly predicted, it is accelerating at the same rate. In 2006 O'Reilly wrote that this technology would "follow the pattern set by earlier disruptions, such as personal computers or instant messaging, and infiltrate organizations in a decentralized, bottom-up fashion, only to become pervasive and essential."[13]

It started with decentralized, ground-up installation of countless wikis, blogs, and forums installed under desks and as IT side projects and now 65% of all companies with 10,000 or more employees have at least "dipped their toe in the water," bearing out the first half of O'Reilly's predictions.[14]

Starting in 2006, software vendors began combining individual social media tools into enterprise-grade Social Business Software which are today rolled out to entire corporations in multi-million dollar deals. Forrester[15] pegs spending on Social Business Software (SBS) in the enterprise at $789 million, projecting growth to \$4.9 billion by 2013. This trend is not limited to any one sector, touching industries across the spectrum, from Banking to Automotive, Consumer Goods to Healthcare, Sporting Goods to Clothing, schools, associations and even the government. O'Reilly noted that the phenomenon of Web 2.0 was unique in that it was being driven by the consumer space first. It is the consumer that will eventually drive these changes into the enterprise, as their "experience with Web 2.0-class software is setting the bar of what software can and should be. Consumers are bringing that knowledge, as well as those expectations, into their roles as corporate employees." Thus the tremendous success of social media in the consumer space, everywhere apparent, will lag but eventually dictate the same change within the enterprise. And this is exactly what we see playing out before our eyes today.

Technology as Culture

Businesses value social media's ability to harness the **collective intelligence** of a large number of users, directly or indirectly. The direct methods are more familiar and easily understood—blogs, wikis, forums, and comments. These are some of the myriad ways social media has empowered individual users to publish and create content that others consume. In the techno world we call this User-Generated Content (UGC). The most successful tools are similar in their simplicity of design, ease of use, and 24/7 availability by multiple means (web, mobile, email) on the Internet. In contrast, there are the indirect methods like book recommendations from Amazon, which draw on the prior actions of millions of users, the similar Genius feature in Apple iTunes, and friend recommendations on Facebook.

Among the direct methods, none has had a greater impact than the blog.

Since 2002, more than 133 million blogs have been created. This is not just a social phenomenon. There is little question that the **blogosphere** has taken a considerable market share of influence from traditional media sources in reporting current events, especially online. In 2008, the Huffington Post and Gizmodo cracked the top ten most visited online news sites. Six blogs logged more than a million unique visitors, and most of the top 10 blogs boasted triple digit annual growth repeated year after year.[16]

The opportunities of these new media have not been restricted to simple conversations among friends. The influence of blogs can be especially pronounced in times of crisis when traditional media alone isn't capable of responding to the scale of the disaster, such as after 9/11 and Hurricane Katrina. Consider this appeal from The Weather Channel:

> Despite having several crews in the field, they can only be in one place at a time, and travel continues to be treacherous. In the meantime, you may use this blog entry as a forum for seeking information about people or places that are important to you.

Similarly, after the tsunami disaster in Southeast Asia on Dec. 26, 2004, blogs not only supplied reporting, but helped people find each other, cope with grief, or find ways to donate money or provide aid.

Blogs also contribute to cultural changes by providing an open forum when traditional media is unable to report freely because of direct governmental control, fear of retribution from advertisers, or other influences. This is routine in countries with official censorship, and was perceptible in the United States in the period following 9/11 and in the beginning of the Iraq War. The influence of social media on politics has only grown since then: in response to the "Tea Party" movement, a "Coffee Party" was proposed on Facebook and has since led to face-to-face gatherings.

The Wiki is another prominent medium of direct UGC, with no more prominent example than Wikipedia. This wiki, an application that enables easy creation and inter-linking of web pages, has over 12 million articles in multiple languages, and is authored, edited, and fact-checked entirely by volunteers, collaboratively, and by anyone who has access to the site. It is a remarkable demonstration of social media turning conventional practice on its head by completely eliminating any central authority. Its vision statement is "Imagine a world in which every single human being can freely share in the sum of all knowledge." Countless wikis have popped up in corporations around the globe to capture knowledge. According to most industry analysts, more than 1/3 of all enterprise has adopted a wiki.

Amazon was one of the first to capitalize on the indirect actions of its users to create valuable new information, such as capturing and showing that "Users who viewed this item eventually bought this." This type of information can be extremely valuable to corporations. In 2008, Netflix ran a competition asking programmers to develop software that does a better job of predicting users' interests in new movies, based on previous selections and the general patterns gathered from Netflix users.

All of this user-generated content reflects what is often called "the wisdom of the crowd."[17] Wikipedia is a perfect example of the "wisdom of the crowd." Its openness to the public allows contributions even from new users who may make only a small change, but aggregated, their contributions have created an entirely new kind of encyclopedia of knowledge. When we consider that this sort of project was once the domain of only the very influential, it's remarkable.

Indirect utilization of UGC can aggregate wisdom even when no one individual has the right answer. In the early 20th century, Sir Francis Galton, an English nobleman and one of the first statisticians, wanted to see how well the public could do at guessing something. He expected that a crowd would be unable to guess the correct weight of an ox. Apparently about 800 people made a guess, and while not one of them was exactly correct, the average of all the guesses was exactly the real weight of the ox. The aggregate of all the guesses was more accurate than any one of the guesses alone, and Galton's calculations showed that the more people who participated and made a guess, the more likely it was that the answer would be as close to right as possible. Businesses are working to take advantage of this phenomenon; shouldn't you?

Social media represents the coming-of-age of Internet technologies that allow people to connect with one another. As these approaches become more and more important in the business world, it's critical for professionals to learn how to use them and use them well. The next chapter will explore the different types of social media and how social media used in part as social business to advance a career as opposed to endanger it.

~chapter two~

The Social Web

When Libby Miller started as an intern for IBM, she was only 22 years old and had zero work experience–this internship was her entrance into the professional world. But with her quick wit and engaging personality, people automatically liked her.

She brought something besides her personality to the table, something that might have been more valuable than her sense of humor and charm. She brought her ability to transform what she learned into readable, consumable blog posts and online documentation. Before the end of her first week, Libby began posting questions on the company forum. She included others by discussing what she was learning. She connected on LinkedIN and Twitter with colleagues she met in the workplace. And she blogged. As her postings became searchable, her coworkers began to notice. Who was this intern who seemed to have such an immediate and far-reaching presence? Libby didn't think twice about her methods of communication–this was second nature to her. She approached her more experienced colleagues about what she viewed as the important technological questions facing the organization. They began to comment and discuss her ideas online.

But Libby didn't stop there. Convinced she was onto something and eager to gain respect for her abilities, she conducted phone and email interviews with a few expert engineers in another department across the country. She summarized their views and reported them online, making the knowledge freely available to everyone in the company. Over the course of a single summer, the unknown, inexperienced intern became a globally-renowned subject-matter expert. When her application for a permanent position hit the candidate lists, it sparked a bidding war: Libby landed job offers from no fewer than six different business units.

Some of the tools Libby used are familiar to most employees. Of course, no one gets too far without job dedication. But Libby took it a few steps further, using these familiar skills and applying them in new ways. Instead of chatting at the water cooler or over lunch, she networked on LinkedIN, Tweeted efficiently, or wrote concise, readable posts for blogs or wikis. Sure, there were plenty of company veterans who were more qualified and more knowledgeable than Libby–after all, she was an intern. But their lack of a digital footprint kept them from making that impression that resulted in future opportunities.

Five years down the road, Libby and her contemporaries will make up nearly half of the workforce. These tech-savvy college grads are less expensive hires because they're inexperienced. Yet some evidence suggests that they may actually be more productive workers because of their digital relationships. In today's era, it's not necessarily what you know, or even whom you know, but rather how quickly you are able to find quality information, especially from the people you consult to make decisions. Social business is creating more tightly knit groups and workers can leverage these groups to perform better than those who insist on flying solo. The McKinsey study showed that high-performing employees have networks that are one third larger than average- and low-performing employees.[1] These larger networks correlate with even larger disparities in productivity. Although high-performing employees may make up less than 20% of a company's workforce, they often account for up to half of its productivity.

In simple terms, workers who draw on larger networks are more productive. They are also team players who are helping their coworkers. By building and participating in these relationships, workers not only gain the tools they need to increase their own productivity, but they provide tools for others in their group to be more productive. Companies are catching onto this trend, and they are using Social Business Software (SBS) to communicate with customers and partners. They are also using it to boost productivity and to keep attrition rates low among their own workers. The Global 1000 companies on this cutting edge include SAP, Lufthansa, Intel, and Nike.

Making the Most from a Crowd

Not to begrudge what your parents told you, but in this day and age, putting your nose to the grindstone and working hard just isn't enough. In order to take advantage of widely-distributed information, you need to network. Without valuable input from others, you are going to find it a challenge to compete in today's technological marketplace.

You can use the same strategies Amazon and Netflix do to process the information gathered from users' patterns of behavior. You can do it by tapping into your own network, and you don't need sophisticated software to reap the benefits!

Think of it this way: If only you and I own a telephone, there's not much value, but the more people who have one, the more useful it becomes. This phenomenon has been quantified by Robert Metcalfe, founder of the Ethernet, who pointed out that a network needs to reach a certain critical mass before users can reap the benefits. The term "network effect" simply means that the usefulness of a networked system increases as more people use it. The actual value of a network is proportional to the square of the number of users. This law applies to most of the common Internet tools in usage today: IM chat, email, blogs, the web.

Exponential Value

Just realizing that there is inherent value in a network is largely intuitive. But when a platform enables users in a network to form their own subgroups, a phenomenon known as Reed's Law[2] goes into effect. Reed described a concept known as group forming. You'll see this concept in action in applications like Squidoo and Bebo. The value produced in these applications is not just perceived; it can scale exponentially. This is because the utility is not bound by the number of users. Instead, the system is developed to handle an infinite number of sub-groups within the network. Math equations aside, you can see this in action on Facebook today, where interest groups are formed on any topic, from science to politics, current events to the arts. To say the implications of Reed's Law are profound would be the understatement of the century. When group-forming networks arrive in your business, to hash out new ideas, to solve problems, and to create inconceivable strides in business, the social business revolution will take off. And, when this happens, creativity and innovation will be the foundation of the New Economy. According to …

[E]ven Metcalfe's Law understates the value created by a group-forming network [GFN] as it grows. Let's say you have a GFN with n members. If you add up all the potential two-person groups, three-person groups, and so on that those members could form, the number of possible groups equals 2n. So the value of a GFN increases exponentially, in proportion to 2n. I call that Reed's Law. And its implications are profound.

You don't have to be a mathematical whiz to understand that network effects is the key that unlocks the door to getting ahead and setting yourself apart. In later chapters, you'll receive practical strategies and guidance for actively taking advantage of these tools as they arrive in your industry. You will learn strategies to manage the value of your personal network that will assist you in everything from making decisions, getting work done, and leading others in ways that will be more successful than anything you imagined before you adopted the notion of the Me Paradox.

The Long Tail

Another key implication of exponential value is the Long Tail. Just as it sounds, good, bad or indifferent, it follows you everywhere. This famous appendage also has a mathematical origin: it's the long, skinny segment of a power law curve distribution (or Pareto distribution), which in economics has traditionally gone unexploited by mass distributors. The popular Long Tail graph represents that 80 percent of the profits come from 20 percent of the products, so a Wal-Mart or the nearly deceased Blockbuster retail chain will generally carry only the top 20 percent.

The economics of Internet sites and modern shipping make it possible for companies like Amazon and Netflix to exploit these neglected segments, by carrying a far larger selection of titles than could be held in any brick-and-mortar store. If you're large enough, all of these little niches add up to a ton of profits. Google's AdSense makes profound use of this as well, by selling ads on the most viewed, most prominent pages, and most frequently-used search terms, right down to the most esoteric phrases, and little-viewed pages. After all, a view is a view and a click is a click, and if Google is there, they're going to make a profit.

Pitfalls of Careless Online Behavior

The Long Tail's effects apply to more than just making money; it can have tremendous benefits when it comes to reputation too. But when used unwisely, one of the Long Tail dangers of the social web reveals itself–too much self revelation.

Privacy and social networking are not mutually exclusive terms, yet there are ways to 'get caught with your pants down' if you're not paying attention. Literally. Take, for example, Ray Lam, a Canadian politician running for election in 2009. As Lam stayed busy running his campaign and promoting his brand of politics, some photos surfaced–embarrassing photos, and not the type that portray a responsible elected official.[3] The first photo showed Lam palming a woman's breast. Another incriminating photo showed Lam with his pants down around his ankles while two people pulled at his underwear. These photos came from Lam's own Facebook page. Someone who was connected to one of his online friends recognized the opportunity, downloaded the photos, and leaked them to the press. CBC Canada broke the news over an April weekend, and on the following Monday, Ray withdrew his candidacy. The photos were probably all in good fun–taken in his freshman year of college for all we know–but his political career was cut short by one bad judgment call.

Lam's party leader said candidates were warned about such possibilities, even regarding material posted on a private page. Ray's Long Tail came back to haunt him. His embarrassing photos may have been only a tiny proportion of the information he had posted online. They may have been taken during one wild and crazy night that didn't define him as a person or a politician; but they were there, just waiting to be exploited. And someone took advantage. Will all politicians now need to be concerned about what they've posted online, all the way back to their adolescent party days? Studies suggest that may indeed be the case, in part because our behavior online is more likely to be problematic than our face-to-face communication.

The Digital Age: Thinking Before Posting

Not only do we present ourselves online different from the way we present ourselves in person, but the differences are mostly negative. One study found that in computer-mediated communication such as social networking, people "may use the computer as a buffer between themselves and others," and that online situations "may weaken the usual bonds of social control."[4]

With weaker social control, psychologists have said that we are bolder and more forthright online. Our outspokenness can create a sense of spilling our guts to an online, unknown audience. And, let's admit it, acting mischievous or venting to what seems to be an anonymous third party feels good. However there's a big downside to consider here. That online, unknown and often-anonymous audience doesn't give us the satisfaction of a response to match our behavior. Because we are getting less and less complex face-to-face interaction, we put more and more of ourselves into our emails and blogs, and here's where the human nature aspect comes into play: The lack of feedback continues to fuel our desires to display ourselves online. It's just a vicious cycle, and just as uncertainty can create errors, putting too much of yourself on the Internet can shatter your career.

While the social norms for the use of social media are still under development, we need to be careful about how much self-revelation we engage in. Think about the early days of email: how many people had a Bible verse in their signature? How many schmaltzy chain mails were being passed around without much consideration? The signals you send when engaging in these kinds of behaviors create a lasting memory, and this memory remains long after norms are established that formalize the boundaries of online behavior. With social media's new possibilities, we need to be cautious about the signals we send now, in the early days of the new technology.

Online Behavior is Still Public Behavior. Be Judicious

Those who have studied online behavior will tell you–too much self-revelation is a social signal of blatant disregard for the status quo. Whether done consciously or sub-consciously, self-revelation has consequences. The consequences of public perception are out of your control once that information has been posted. Research shows that the public perceives comments derived from this self revelation as coming from someone who is either completely assured of his status (does not require future consideration), or intends for others to see him as disruptive or unreliable.[5] These aren't good perceptions for potential employers or other business contacts to have about you. Instead, they are viewed as warning signs, indicators that someone is not going to make a reliable, productive, cooperative colleague–or a responsible politician.

The "network" aspect of social networking also means that the behavior of the people you associate with will reflect on you. All those things your parents told you about your reputation remain true in the online world: be careful whom you associate with, more friends are not necessarily always better, and friends' behaviors have implications for your reputation. Of course, you want to take advantage of networking to make beneficial connections, but your online networking, like your in-person networking, needs to be actively managed and done judiciously.

Privacy: What does it Mean?

One anonymous person commenting on the Ray Lam incident wrote that "For anyone over thirty, all this self-revelation [needed for online social networking] is too much information." At the very least, it's embarrassing. At the very worst, and Ray Lam had to learn the hard way, it could be compromising. A majority of adults still believe in the value of privacy which, at its simplest, means you get to control what different people know about you. That simple definition of privacy is no longer applicable. Whatever privacy means in the digital age, it's definitely *not* that you control what others know.

Have you tried searching your own name on Google? What about zabasearch.com? That publicly available engine offers some fairly detailed information to people who are willing to pay a few dollars for it. With tools like these available, you don't control your own information anymore. The government sector is also increasing the transparency of our daily lives. You've heard about big brother. Well, he might not be watching you, in particular, but he's watching, and you don't want to be caught with your pants down, so to speak. Just ask Ray Lam.

Technology is Invasive

In 2008, the New York City police department announced that it was adding 100 video cameras in lower Manhattan.[6] This effort was aimed at getting license-plate numbers for traffic-law purposes, but it's just another example of how information about us isn't always ours to keep private.

The spread of information isn't just restricted to individuals. Google's *Street View* service provides relatively current photographs of street scenes in major cities alongside its regular map information. The views can help you recognize the building where you're meeting a friend for lunch, but they can also show people heading into an adult book store or, worse yet, create a false alarm.

In 2001, in Tampa, Florida, police began using facial recognition software to catch wanted criminals. Not one criminal was ever caught as part of the program, which was abandoned two years later after much controversy. But the software created false alarms by picking up on faces that seemed to match but didn't. On at least one occasion, both police and a Tampa man wound up embarrassed. Rob Milliron, then 32, showed up on a surveillance camera while lunching in Ybor City. In 2008, Tampa police used his photo to demonstrate the system to local news media. According to the St. Petersburg Times, a Tulsa, Oklahoma, woman saw his picture and identified him as her ex-husband who just happened to be wanted on felony child neglect charges. Three police officers showed up at Milliron's construction job site, asking if he was the wanted man. Turns out he had never married, never had kids, never even been to Oklahoma.

Effort is Required to Regain Control

Reality is, more of our lives are being recorded and captured, and the possible recourse for all this archived information is increasingly risky, regardless of whether we participate or not.

Google announced that it will limit access to images taken outside women's crisis shelters to minimize the risk that abusive spouses will find their victims, but there's always the possibility of unwelcome revelations in every image.

Despite our inherent beliefs about privacy, the fact of the matter is that we've never had absolute control over our personal information. We fill out government forms, stores use surveillance to prevent shoplifting, people see each other on the street, and overhear things at work. But using social media creates a whole new class of interactions–and these are easily made available to the masses with the click of a mouse.

A conversation that might be forgotten in a day is stored electronically, creating an unexpected permanence to each and every comment by you or about you. As Daniel Solove remarked in his book *Future of Reputation,*[7] "what was once scattered, localized, and forgettable is now permanent and searchable." Even when a website changes its look, its content, and its appearance, the older form is often available: see archive.org and its *Wayback Machine* for accessing stored copies of older versions of websites. Admittedly, only a tiny number of Facebook scandals make the headlines, especially compared to the number of users. Material posted and removed last month may come back next year to haunt the not-so-cautious user.

Making Responsible Choices

In the past, limitations on our control of information about ourselves made us develop tenets or rules. We had the good sense not to get drunk at the company Christmas party and tell the boss we detest him. With the changing availability of information through the social web, we should continue to think of privacy not just as secrecy. We can be fairly open and still maintain a level of privacy. We just need to develop new strategies for the types of information we make available in certain areas.

Right now, more and more people are using Facebook for business. It has easy and fun tools (such as games and better 'groups' functionality), and a huge number of people already have pages. It has far outdone LinkedIN as a networking tool. That doesn't mean Facebook will be the one and only professional networking medium, but it indicates the direction in which things are moving. Even with its inherent dangers, refusing to participate in business that has gone online and social will result in workers being left behind.

There are definite advantages to using social media for professional purposes. More people are reached; relationships are strengthened. The combination of professional and social information gives a more holistic view of a person. And sharing just one or two personal experiences, interests, or emotions can humanize a professional relationship and make a connection that much stronger. With the social web, privacy is not about controlling information. It's about managing the sum of information about you for the sake of your reputation.

A Well-Cultivated Reputation is Key

These days, we find that the Internet is the place to be, but it's also a place that never forgets. 'Less is more' is a good motto to remember.

In a popular October 2004 article in *Wired Magazine*, Chris Anderson popularized the concept "Long Tail" to describe pieces of information that get only a few exposures each, but they follow you nonetheless. In the publishing world, these are obscure titles with small print runs, not the latest Harry Potter book. But Amazon makes a substantial amount of its profit off of the Long Tail because it has created an economical way to sell multitudes of those obscure titles—sure, just a few of each individual title get sold, but the profits add up.

Use the Long Tail to build your reputation in a similar way. Every professionally oriented interaction may only make an impression on a few people. Think about this as compared to one unprofessional interaction that becomes the talk of your department. The Long Tail of small benefits is where your reputation—and your career—will profit.

Less is More–Start Small

The permanence of online material is not the only reason why the *Less is More* mentality is important on the social web. There's also the accessibility of online information. Personal connections support relationships, but if that information is accessible to others, it has the potential to create a very different impression. Suppose that you're using Facebook to be in touch with a coworker while both of you are pregnant. By making one comment about the trials of finding work-appropriate maternity clothes may be fine; a sarcastic threat to wear your ugliest maternity jeans to the next board meeting might make a future employer think twice about your professionalism. Never mind that your colleague knew you were only kidding–and that you looked stunning at the meeting–even something that is appropriate in the context of one relationship can appear totally different without that context.

If you think potential employers would never look at a social networking site to help make a determination about your candidacy, you're wrong. In an August 2009 study by Harris Interactive, 45 percent of employers who responded said they looked up information about job candidates on the social web. This is more than double the percent of employers that reported doing similar checks in 2008. And, recent findings indicate that employers are taking action on the basis of what they find: 35 percent of them turned down a candidate, especially if the material included racy photos or references to drinking and drug use.[8] Some companies considered gratuitous negative discussion of a prior job or colleague a warning sign, and even evaluated candidates' online communication skills.

Whenever you post something, treat it as if it will be viewed by a future interviewer–because it probably will be. Your online reputation is part of the foundation of your career, and just like the foundation for your dream house, the foundation for your dream career should be as solid as you can make it. You don't have to destroy all evidence of your personality online. That can also be damaging–making you a less-attractive candidate. Just be judicious about what you say and how much you say: less is more. Start with less and slowly add to it until you reach the desired results. Make sure to give yourself enough time for feedback along the way. The Long Tail means that your gradual efforts will add up to big benefits for you.

Using Social Business to Enhance Reputation

The social web multiplies the opportunities for both good and bad developments as we connect online. The very ideas of privacy and professionalism are different in the new paradigm of social business. What to put online and how to present it are key issues for individuals as well as companies. Ignoring these developments is like trying to steer a runaway train–it's too easy to lose control. You want to be able to direct the development of your online reputation, and by participating in the conversations going on about you, and by engaging with these new tools in the right way, you can establish an online reputation that will take you to the top of your field. Creating and managing an online reputation is an evolving exercise. Your reputation is like a company's brand. It establishes a basis for the exchange of social capital that gives you a tremendous advantage. The later chapters walk you through the steps to developing your reputation positively and proactively.

Reputation as a Valuable Commodity

How many times have you watched TV shows or movies where a powerful government official or major mafia boss said, "I'm going to have to call in a favor to make this work?" It always seemed that important people were able to get favors because the consequences of refusal would be so severe. Fear appeared to be the element that convinced others to grant the kind of favors that helped those in power maintain their positions. But once you understand how reputations operate you will realize that fear was not the basis of these interactions.

A schoolyard bully may be able to get by based on the fear he creates; but in the adult world, powerful and influential figures use an exchange system based on reputation. These exchanges need to flow both ways in order to get things accomplished.

When it works, these exchanges have the power to create a memorable reputation. Mafia-type organizations have known this for a long time. One example lies with the Yakuza, sometimes called the Japanese mafia. Over a decade ago, there was a very destructive earthquake in Kobe, Japan. The Yakuza were proactive and expeditious in providing emergency care and provisions. The government, on the other hand, lagged behind in its response and, in turn, was criticized for its lack of preparedness. To this day, Nagata Ward is no longer the poorest neighbor of the city of Kobe, and it remains a stronghold for the Yakuza. The people there are amazingly loyal to this violent, illegal organization, because of the reputation the Yakuza gained from that one event.

This was a consistent strategy for the Yakuza. Before the earthquake, the group had immersed themselves in the community, trying to create a reputation of being good citizens. But their behavior, which was not always obvious, was contradicted by news reports of their violence and bad character. This created an inconsistent message, where people never knew if the Yakuza would stop giving and simply start taking. The community was unable to fully trust the Yakuza and include them in the social exchange system, and thus in the life of the community.

The earthquake created a unique situation for the Yakuza, and they were able to display a symbolic and practical activity which created a lasting impression based on one overwhelmingly positive incident. These unusual opportunities do occur, but more often a good reputation is based on consistency. The Yakuza weren't able to achieve that consistency before the earthquake, but in one single action they changed their image.

Consistency + Confidence = Currency

Once the Yakuza had a reputation based on something other than fear, the community could begin to trust them in to having a reciprocal relationship, which enables all kinds of exchanges. Consistency creates an idea of reliability in a reciprocal relationship. This mindset reduces the participants' risks by increasing their confidence in each other. That confidence relies on the idea that a reputation is valuable and that value will be honored and protected. Reputation, and the confidence it creates, become the pillars of social exchange. Building a solid reputation will open up new avenues of opportunity and success.

Reputation is based on the perception of the community (those within a network), thus the visibility of related exchanges help determine its value. The Yakuza's opportunity after the earthquake was important because that positive interaction was visible. Many people needed serious help, and everyone knew who had provided it. This direct knowledge outweighed the people's indirect knowledge of the Yakuza's other activities. Visibility often doesn't outweigh consistency, but it's important to make the consequence of exchanges visible for both parties.

Why Consistency Matters

An accumulation of small positive efforts will prepare you to take advantage of a unique opportunity that provides great visibility and enhances your reputation; that is the Long Tail in action. In contrast, something negative that has little visibility or is only known about indirectly is much less likely to damage the reputation of parties in an exchange. Trust and reciprocity go hand-in-hand. The loss of confidence, either through breaking the rules of the exchange or a serious change in reputation from some other infraction, is what destroys the ability to participate socially. Building the kind of consistency that comes from small, repeated actions keeps that confidence high.

Reputations are unusual things: they are 'sticky', or durable, because they are usually based on consistency, on the Long Tail of built-up evidence about a person or a corporation. But reputations are also fragile–a single negative event that is directly known about by everyone can shatter a good reputation. How can something be both fragile and durable? It's certainly a paradox. Anyone can create a reputation. Understanding it and managing it is part of the Me Paradox.

RESEARCH SUMMARY

Here's another interesting paradox. You don't need to be an extrovert to develop a robust reputation. For some people, the most challenging part of the Me Paradox is the inherent difficulty of interacting with others. Some people are natural socializers who have loads of charisma and love interacting with people. These extroverts have traditionally been regarded as having an advantage in the business world. But the process of establishing an online reputation has many features that favor introverts, those individuals who find social interactions to be draining or slightly uncomfortable. In fact, everyone trying to use social media ought to study some introverts' traits and take advantage of them.

Psychologist Carl Jung's work popularized the terms "introvert" and "extrovert," but it was the Myers-Briggs Type Indicator (MBTI), developed in the 1940s, that turned it into a household word. The MBTI operationalized Jung's work into a personality test that allowed people to gauge themselves on a scale of introverted to extroverted, along with other major personality characteristics. The MBTI's questions and scale indicate that there are many different kinds of introverts and extroverts: some are more analytical, some more emotional, some left-brained and some right-brained. In fact, everyone is a mix of introverted and extroverted attitudes, and individuals are often extroverted in some situations and introverted in others. So the whole idea of introvert vs. extrovert is more a general tendency than a hard-and-fast set of rules about personality or behavior. The quality that generally identifies the inherently introverted types is that they tend to feel like social interactions require a deliberate effort.

This sense of effort means that introverts often feel like outsiders in an extroverts' world. Introverts may be a minority–from 15 to 25 percent of the total population.[9] But they are a significant minority in the 40 and over population, up to 50 percent, statistics show.[10] In the business world, introverts often feel even that they are at a disadvantage. Part of working smarter is using human relationships to your advantage, working with your allies to improve your position. In the past, introverts were often admonished to look at the successes gained by others through networking and self-marketing. This is largely because they described themselves by stating, "I don't like talking to people," "It just feels so fake to me," or "I don't have anything to prove."

Recognizing our Tendencies

Introverts really do think and function differently in social situations. The good news is that qualities that were formerly seen as handicaps now position introverts to take the best advantage of the social web's new paradigms.

Put simply, introverts prefer depth. They have fewer friends, but they are quite close to their friends. Just as they like to know people very well, introverts are often subject matter experts who tend to be very knowledgeable about a particular topic, possibly a very specialized one. They are reflective, and they internalize new ideas more quickly. But this reflective style means that they don't converse as quickly as others. They're thinking before speaking, while extroverts more often "think out loud," or talk out their ideas as they are formed. Offline, an introvert's different conversational style might be viewed as awkward or geeky, because it isn't based on the charisma that is so prized in face-to-face interactions. It's not that introverts are anti-social, it's that the mismatch in thinking and speaking styles–especially in terms of timing–makes them seem awkward to extroverts, who, with their fast-talking style, perpetuate and enforce that image. But online, it's a whole new world for introverts. The awkwardness is eased tremendously, so the introvert's expert knowledge of a particular medium gets a chance to shine, and others can benefit from their extensive specialization as well. An introvert's brilliant contribution, solving a major problem in just a short forum post or blog entry, doesn't need to depend on charisma, but instead on the quality of work to gain reputation.

Although the introvert's tendency to form fewer but closer relationships is a burden, it can also be a benefit online. Reputations are built on people's mindsets and opinions, so you can't have a reputation without people. But the type of people you build ties with also influences others' opinions of you. Being a close contact of the President is going to carry a different kind of weight in shaping your reputation than being a close contact of your neighbors. Having more contacts is good for your reputation, but having the *right contacts* is more important.

Introverts' habit of thinking before speaking also means that they project a controlled and consistent message, which I have seen is a fundamental pillar of reputation building. Now, being online instead of face-to-face doesn't mean no one is listening–quite the opposite! A recent article in the Wall Street Journal titled, *How Facebook Can Ruin Your Friendships* talked about "Facebook fatigue" that comes from being overloaded with too much trivial information from friends who post constantly. Psychology Professor Patricia Wallace pointed out that the feedback would normally give extroverts the clue to 'take a break' is missing: "Online, people can't see the yawn." Here's where an introvert's normal habits come in handy again. In Marti Olsen Laney's 2002 book, *The Introvert's Advantage: How to Thrive in an Extrovert World,[11]* she describes the "mind/vapor lock" which requires introverts to take a break and shut the mind down when over-stimulated. The constant online conversations can swiftly cause us to become over stimulated, and it is all too easy to react hastily and do something we might later regret. The introvert's tendency to shut down for a while is an advantage in these situations. Extroverts who understand the landscape can manage equally well online, but their tendency to react quickly is self-defeating in situations where the feedback mechanism is slower and less precise than face-to-face communications. The context of an online exchange is harder to read. This is in large part, due to the lack of nuances and nonverbal cues. As a consequence, an extrovert's quick reaction is more likely to make a mistake through poor word choice or an inappropriate tone that might be misconstrued. Professor Wallace advised people to avoid those yawn-inducing posts online by taking time to think it through: "Run it by that focus group of one." A solid handle on these ideas means that you can reap the benefits of both introverts' and extroverts' thinking. Reach out to others, and take time along the way to internalize a response simultaneously, getting the best of both worlds.

The Role of Reputations

Reputation is a word most of us are familiar with, but defining it creates more of a challenge. The word comes from the Latin word for a consideration or an estimate that has developed through time. The definition used by both business and academia is:

Reputation is the estimation of consistency over time of an attribute of an entity.

The word "entity" is deliberately vague. Almost anyone or anything can have a reputation these days. Traditionally, businesses talk about brands and branding referring only to physical customer goods. These days, a brand is anything that can be offered to a market for attention, acquisition, use, or consumption. In essence, anything that might satisfy a need or want. Any brand has a reputation, so in today's world we use the term "entity" to include a physical good, a service, a store, a person, an organization, a place, or even an idea that has a reputation.

A reputation is used as a means of inferring the quality or qualities of that person. Is your cubicle neighbor friendly? What does that make you think about her? A reputation is established by the flow of information from one person to another, and there is latency built into the process. In spite of the fact that it's not an instant reward, a reputation is an extremely valuable resource to have. One CEO described reputation as "a strategic tool to create business opportunities, mitigate threats, and manage risk."[12]

The Intangible Weapon of Choice

Despite their paradoxical nature, reputations are strategic tools. They are sometimes difficult to understand because they defy the usual paradigms of balancing risk and reward. At the beginning, a reputation looks like a bad investment, because it requires you to act repeatedly, and solely on the faith of future rewards after a considerable time lag. But this is why a reputation is a smart investment. If you understand the role of consistency in creating and maintaining a reputation, you will realize how little cost is involved in this investment that offers hefty rewards in the future.

Sometimes, the role of reputation gets ignored because the costs and rewards are hard to quantify. Nationally and internationally, there is a great deal of disagreement over the valuation of intangible assets such as a reputation. A reputation is based on consideration, on estimates, which are almost impossible to calculate. This intangible quality is what makes reputation a difficult subject to teach in business schools. It gets a lot of lip service, but not much is said in mainstream society about creating or managing reputation.

Reputations are about the consistency of attributes. These attributes can include kind, friendly, skillful, smart, useful, etc. For a professional reputation the attributes fall into roughly four areas:

- **Differentiation**, or distinctiveness in the marketplace
- **Relevance** to a particular situation
- **Esteem**, or perceived quality and popularity
- **Knowledge**, or what the entity stands for

Displaying any one of these attributes consistently is what it takes to establish a reputation. Do you smile at your cubicle neighbor? The receptionist? Do you do it daily? It doesn't cost anything to repeat positive actions that help build your reputation. So, while a reputation may seem hard to understand or quantify in words, it is easy to create.

Practice on those around you, and see what consistency can do for your reputation.

Measurement Beyond Faith

Reputation doesn't work on a numerical scale. It works on a scale from no reputation to more reputation: positive or negative. If you send mixed and confusing signals, these signals cancel each other out and leave you with no reputation. No one wants to associate with an unknown quantity with whom others don't want to interact. Research shows that having a consistently positive reputation is best, of course, but a consistently negative reputation is still advantageous over mixed signals. Let's face it, people want to be around people who are consistent and reliable–good or bad (of course, to a point). They prefer working with them, as a known quantity, because it makes work easier.

Management guru Jeffrey Pfeffer has repeatedly argued that personal reputation is an integral part of how power and influence are acquired and used effectively. Florida State University Psychology Professor Gerald Ferris described this process in terms of decision, latitude, and autonomy. Individuals with a positive reputation are likely to have more autonomy and less monitoring than those who are held in low regard. A good reputation makes you better able to do your job, and that pays off in results.

This is where the Me Paradox offers tremendous opportunities. The process in this book helps you make small changes to your activities that will build your reputation, giving you the potential for huge benefits. Compare these costs and benefits; and then you'll have your own personal evidence on why learning how to engage in social business is worth your time.

Online Reputation

For a long time, reputation seemed to be something that only executives, politicians, and sales personnel worried about. They were practically the only ones who cared about a reputation since they were the only people required to be recognized by name. The Internet changes the dynamics of reputation. Now everybody's reputation matters, and we have to cope with the accompanying paradigm shift. This book emphasizes the way that shift affects your activities, but with the right tools and strategies, it's pretty easy to adapt. You can succeed by just tweaking a few of your methods to create and manage your online reputation for the best advantage to your character.

One of the biggest changes the Internet has brought about so far is that it makes society more participatory. People not only expect, but also demand to be involved in conversations about everything: companies, doctors, professors, consumer goods, and YOU. Your customers, your peers, your suppliers, and your partners are now talking, and at some point they will end up talking about you. Those conversations are how reputations are made and spread, whether it's with information from performance reviews, peer reviews, surveys, or just the latest chatter. With more and more conversations taking place all the time, everybody and everything is being talked about, so everybody and everything has a reputation. Information about your brand is spreading, and it will come back to either haunt you or reward you.

Before now, only whole companies had enough riding on their reputations to put real effort into studying them, creating them, and managing them. The techniques used by big business can apply to individuals, but there are also a lot of new situations for individuals to think about in the context of the social web. Companies often focused on creating reactions, sending out messages, and protecting their profile or reputation. The participatory nature of the Internet means that you can do so much more with the tools available. Like other brands, you must participate in the social web.

Profile vs. Reputation

Your profile is only the beginning. It's what you control, what you build, and write, and put out there. Furthermore, your reputation is what others think, their consideration of you. And, that, my friends, is based on much more than just what you say about yourself–good and bad included. Your reputation is the sum of what you say in addition what everyone else says, in addition to the interactions people have with you, and any content you post online. It also includes all that gets said through accidents, mistaken identity problems, confusion, and so on. It includes times when the online world and offline world don't quite match up as well. Some of it is out of your direct control, but you can steer it in the right direction if you understand the environment you're operating in.

Managing your profile and how you interact with others gives you a certain degree of control over your reputation as a whole. But to really take advantage of the phenomenon, you have to understand the landscape. Think of the difference between a movie star who is popular and respected as opposed to one who is always on the front cover of the tabloids. They may both be famous and be working in the same landscape, but one of them understands that landscape and the other doesn't understand, or doesn't care. To create and manage your online reputation, it helps to understand the online reputation lifecycle.

Online Reputation Lifecycle

The lifecycle is not as complicated as it sounds. As shown in figure 2-1, the three (3) parts to the lifecycle include your presence, your network, and your engagement.

Figure 2-1

ONLINE REPUTATION LIFECYCLE

Presence

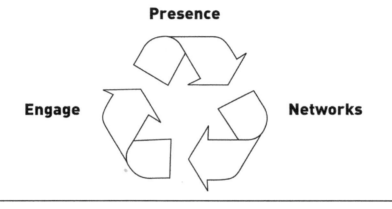

Engage   **Networks**

The Who: Presence

Even if you're a veteran in your field, creating an online presence is the first step. In order to integrate yourself into any group or establish exchanges, people need to know who you are. We're social beings, after all, and we behave very differently depending on the person we're dealing with. It's much easier to be accommodating with someone we know than with an abstraction, like a screen name or an avatar. Establishing your presence is a matter of preparing a story of who you are and what you do. It is a baseline for growth; it creates confidence and prepares you for the consistency that is so important to developing your reputation. As you progress and your online reputation develops, you will update your presence to reflect that growth and evolution.

The Where: Network

The growth of your reputation comes about not just because of what you say in your profile, but where you act and speak, and with whom you interact and speak. That's your network. It's not just an online community or your friends list, it's all the places where you have the option of participating. That can be a blog, an industry news publication, forums–basically anything that is associated with your name–your brand, which makes it important to choose the right network for your purposes.

Different networks can serve different goals, so you need to evaluate them and match them to your purpose. Your network is defined by what kinds of groups and technologies you're in touch with, and how those relate to your industry and goals. For example, Facebook is not where you want to establish the heart of your online reputation. It's simply not a professional place where you want to lay a stake in your professional future. Then again, LinkedIN isn't the place you want to be either. While it's not a bad idea to have a profile and a presence there, it's too static to create meaningful connections and really get yourself out there. LinkedIN is mostly still a job-search oriented tool and not a comprehensive exchange where information and relationships are earned. Thankfully, there are plenty of other resources–and new ones are constantly developing. These are places specific to your interests or industry–where you can network more actively and professionally

The How: Engagement

Once you have established a presence and chosen the right networks, you get to begin to strategically engage: selecting where to participate, when, and with whom, so that your engagement develops your online reputation and your professional life to the fullest. You want a reputation that people trust, that they can rely on. In addition, you want to make sure valuable content is associated with your brand, so that when someone searches for you, they find useful material, and when someone sees valuable content, they begin to remember your brand alongside it. That two-way connection is at the heart of establishing a reputation that is not just about your personality but about your value proposition.

As this cycle continues, you'll need to update your presence and continue to reevaluate your networks on the basis of the growth you've gained. Maybe your profile updates include a well thought-out success story, a blurb about your new degree, a review or description of training you recently attended, or a new skill you've mastered. As your goals develop, you might think about shifting to a different network. This kind of growth is how your online reputation goes from being just a lifeless profile to a way of working that will carry you all the way to the top.

~chapter three~

Understanding Online Presence

Yesterday it was Twitter, today it's Google Buzz...and day after day, week after week, it continues.

We are all trying to keep up with the technology. As we build this online reputation, it helps to start slow and keep a steady pace. We will match our stride with the growth of the information in our area of expertise, and not necessarily with the technology.

As you think about your profile content, think in terms of a 'less is more" approach. Within that approach, we will use the means available to us and stay focused on our goals, working our way toward them through repetition and consistency. Risk is not the enemy, but rather the key ingredient for the recipe of success; and, like salt, you need to sprinkle to taste because, once poured, you can't turn back.

The Time is Now

The Internet is the greatest tool available for the average person. What else costs less than $50 dollars per month but allows a single individual to create a grand empire? Take, for example, the creator of the popular dating website, plentyoffish.com; the creator makes over $10 million dollars a year with a web product he fashioned in his spare time. This is an opportunity that can't be ignored. It is a wise time to begin to use the Internet and SBS creatively and passionately. We have only skimmed the surface of what is possible on the Internet and technology in general, which leaves a world, and beyond, of possibilities.

We all have assumptions of what we can achieve, technologies we trust, unique circumstances, and distinct opinions on what works or what doesn't. These should not be discounted. In fact, we can make our instincts work for us by cataloging them, understanding our reasoning behind certain decisions, and getting a vibe for how these incremental steps move us toward our wants and desires.

Now that you have the philosophy and a good understanding of working within the Me Paradox to create and manage your reputation, let's move onto the other tools, skills, and methods to get the job done. These techniques are founded on best practices and experiences, but your own unique situation will come into play as you make decisions about practices that work best for you, especially as it pertains to the implementation and the networks you choose. There is no 'one-size-fits-all' approach.

The Presence Phase

In order to be *present* in the online world, you need to capture your identity and lay the foundation that defines your online presence. Publishing your characteristics is the chance to show who you are by building your reputation and brand. Whether you are an introverted expert or an extroverted novice, your presence begins with a profile and the places where that profile lives.

- Define your presence with a profile and a home(s) for it
- Establish your reputation by publishing characteristics
- Don't forget the old adage, 'less is more'
- Take the bull by the proverbial horns and be upfront: By trying to maintain privacy, you might be letting others establish your reputation for you

Brand Identity

Many marketing folks would say your profile is your brand identity, the referable portion of your signal. You control the message and direct the perception it creates. Adding content, commenting on content, and cultivating relationships are core participation activities, but without an online presence they amount to wasted energy.

Profile and presence are similar but different. Online presence is the compilation of multiple profiles and identity markers. At the very basic level, your profile is what you control. You build it, post it, and update it. It allows a user to communicate their personal and professional details to all other users within a network.

As you might be aware, you probably have at least one profile on the web somewhere. Some of it, you have no control over, but it all stands out like a Yellow Pages ad when someone searches your name. The uncontrollable profiles are created when public documents, such as a property deed or mortgage records, are made available online or when automated programs go on search-and-compile missions so they can charge people for publicly available information about you. Zoominfo is just one example of a site like this. The compilation of these pieces, along with the information you control, become your personal advertisement and eventually your online reputation.

Your profile is the seed; your online reputation is what sprouts from that seed. The Me Paradox involves planting a seed that can grow in the direction of your passions and objectives.

Setting up a profile is an exercise in self-revelation. It requires walking a very fine line. Just as there are issues with too much self disclosure, there are also dangers in too little exposure. Developing a reputation and participation in social business requires you to be known and discoverable. It's impossible to be a fanatic about maintaining your privacy and still be successful in this new economy.

Balance Privacy to Your Advantage

Privacy comes with a disclaimer: it makes people curious. Others will exert more effort when they think you're trying to keep quiet. Instead, take on a filtering mentality. Filtering is about being present to the degree of your choosing, and funneling only the most relevant information. This mindset helps you not get caught up in the privacy trap–that rabbit hole you slip into when the attempt to keep a few things to yourself becomes a game for others who are trying to find them. Remember to use your resources wisely and join only the networks that will benefit you, then use scrutiny when deciding how much and the types of information you reveal within them.

Filtering Prevents Information Overload and More...

The ease of publishing online coupled with the ever-increasing level of **SPAM** makes it a bigger challenge to discover and know what's important. Whom do we trust for information: CNN, Fox News, Christian Science Monitor, Wikipedia? Factor in personal tastes, technology, experiences, the rapid change of industry and business, and now, we have a dynamic and complex problem when it comes to gathering information specific to our unique needs.

Our participation and our activity, when shared, help us filter this information for each other within our personal networks. But only if we participate. For instance, you may bookmark a site you trust, say, on how to make proper footnotes, thus making life easier for another person in your network. Now this contact, because of your participation, may not need to use their deduction powers to find the most reliable source. This subtlety is online reputation management and it is the Me Paradox in action. By helping others, you help yourself. And, the filtering dynamic allows you to no longer have to evaluate every single piece of information.

You have also found a way, within your profile, to stand out from the crowd. For instance, you are a Red Sox fan who designs billboard graphics. By adding this information to your profile, not only will Red Sox fans in the network find you, but users seeking someone with expertise in billboard graphics will find you as well. Think of the filtering mentality as one that enables you to avoid having to sift through mountains of information to find what you need. When we filter, we are making others' lives easier and creating more potential for our own profits–filtering works for both information that comes in and information that goes out.

Balancing Tips

At the 2009 CES conference, a group of attendees interested in the social web conversed on the importance of having an online professional and personal profile, and the implications in the offline world. Here are their thoughts:

> People are using Facebook for business on an increasing basis. This is indicative of some sort of shift, but it does not mean everyone will now be doing professional networking on Facebook. The shift might be technical (access more users, ease of use) or it might be behavioral (less separation between professional and personal, which is been accepted by more and more people). There are definitely advantages to sharing professional and social info with one's connections gives a better way to broadcast your message to many people, and strengthen your online presence and relationships. Plus, it gives a more holistic view of a person.

As you might gather from this summary, for business professionals, the important take away is the profile information mix: A connection between two or more people is stronger when they share a personal experience, interest or emotion.

So, where do you draw the line? How do you give enough personal information to build relationships yet maintain a professional profile and reputation?

A few guideposts to keep in mind:

- **When in doubt, leave it out.** If you are questioning how much to self-reveal, err on the side of caution.
- **Just like in real life, think before you speak.** Be judicious with what you say and how much you say.
- **Start small.** Begin with less and stay relative to your comfort level and in line with the level of exposure of others within the network.
- **Build slowly and gradually,** adding content until you reach the desired results.
- **Be sure you allow enough time to allow for feedback.** There is a time lag here.

Context Matters

Different rules apply for different professions. For instance, a tutor or a nanny may do fine with using a Facebook profile for business networking. In this line of work, posting pictures of their children or others they have cared for would be acceptable. But individuals need to use discretion about the types of information they provide, and this discretion needs to be dependent on the industry they are in. For instance, a journalist does not want to include information in her profile that gives an impression of bias or political favor, especially if she covers politics. It would be instant death to her career. A filtering mindset is a reflective exercise–you need to ask yourself how the information you put in your profile correlates to the type of information and people your profile attracts. Are these the people who will help you achieve your goals and objectives?

When putting up a profile in a network where a resume is more appropriate, LinkedIN, for example, you might seek input from others in your network to get ideas on the protocols for your particular field or industry. For instance, a freshly graduated lawyer might ask a peer or colleague to review his resume and offer comments. This approach works regardless of your profession and the particular network you are in. A graphic artist in an online group tailored to his profession might seek out a random review from his peers. And, a nanny might ask for suggestions about which Facebook groups to join to help grow her home daycare business.

Profile First, Engage Later

The online reputation lifecycle in **Chapter 2** encourages you to present first and engage later. In other words, without an online presence, any signals that you communicate will be unheard or met with resistance.

The Internet and even your online community or network is a vast space. You cannot control everything that gets put online, the way people will react to you, or how technology will perceive and react to your participation. However, managing your profile, how you interact or don't interact, your goals and your connections, and your networks give you the power to manipulate this phenomenon to a certain degree–this is why it is so powerful and becomes an immediate competitive advantage for those who comprehend and wield it.

Knowing Yourself

User profiles provide information about yourself for others online. The type of profile information entered determines the context for interaction. Most often the owner of the website determines what profile fields will be used. No one can stop you from turning your profile into a professional one, regardless of the website it resides in. However, the effectiveness of business profiles on Facebook is still a matter of debate in most industries.

A robust business profile will allow professionals to interact through business-oriented characteristics and attributes. This setup allows professionals and entrepreneurs to connect with each other and search for resources/contacts/partners by location, expertise, or any profile field. And professionals and entrepreneurs can do so with confidence, knowing that the community or the system has vetted that profile, providing a highly reliable signal.

On the flip side, you can create a social profile anywhere; choose wisely. If your Plaxo profile talks about your lovely long eyelashes it would probably be more effective on plentyoffish.com. Social profiles are built on the personal information of the site's members, especially those who participate and contribute. These social profiles can contain fields that range from relationship status to religion and even to sexual orientation. This information is then shared with members' friends and the variant degrees of separation via social media.

When choosing to have a profile within an online community or social networking site, try to notice what type of questions and profile attributes they are collecting. Remember, websites will have different viewing capabilities depending on a reduced profile, connection- or relationship-oriented profile view, and even paid membership views, making it important to keep the distinction between business and personal.

Knowing the Network

Your profile and your activity are roommates. They both live in a network and work together to determine signal strength. The information you put in your profile should reflect the technology features of the network. As for any online community or networking site, basic features for user searching and profile browsing are permitted and offer a wide range of community building primitives. For a site like LinkedIN, it may be necessary to differentiate yourself from the crowd. If you're one of a dozen real estate agents, then the information and connections you put up may make a big difference. In a more tight-knit group, though, purpose as well as historical content help to determine whether to trust another user. The emphasis is not purely on profile attributes, but on merit, association, and participation within that network–your activity within the network.

In an SBS network like Intel OpenPort,[1] you can keep your profile simple, but you will want to use buzzwords and keywords in your "expertise" description. Your work experience could be just the name of the company and/or job title. This is an example of when your reputation will depend more on your participation and the content you create than what is in your profile.

Knowing Your Core Values

As you establish a stronger online presence, you will almost certainly be involved in more than one network, but be careful not to catch online schizophrenia by having varied profiles on different networks. It is not hard to imagine peers, prospective business partners, clients, and employers checking multiple networks to learn more about you for a more comprehensive view. And now with websites like pipl.com, it becomes as easy as a click of a button to consolidate a profile. The general essence, the theme of who you are, must transcend any specific site. For instance, if you are known for a particular expertise or for your loyalty, show that in various ways. Make sure that you don't express that you are loyal in one profile and then focus on being creative in another without hints of loyalty sprinkled throughout, especially if loyalty is your defining characteristic. Find one trait that is undeniably you and then make sure that trait is emphasized in every online profile you have. This gives the differentiation of profile variations based on the network your profile resides in, yet it provides the foundation needed to maintain a consistent brand identity, or signal.

Empower Your Online Profile

There are a wide range of different approaches to developing your profile. Some believe it should be a variant of your resume and some believe it should be purely an elevator pitch–short and sweet.

Regardless of which school of thought you align with, think about your online profile as a balancing act.

Your profile is also an accumulation of your references, and the feedback you receive from others through ratings and testimonials, or more fundamentally, the use of the **Warranting Principle**. Developed by Joseph Walther and Malcolm Parks,[2] the principle summarizes why what others say, especially those with no incentives or stake in what is being talked about, is worth much more than the material generated by those who do have a stake in and a say about it. The concept is simple to understand, but tougher to put in practice–at least when done ethically.

Trust Development Mechanism

Isaac Sweeney, a writer and editor, is a member of oDesk, a site that matches people or companies with certain task needs to contractors willing to perform those tasks. Isaac has experience and knowledge, but still his first oDesk job was hard to come by. He had built a profile–the first step–and he bid on projects that he was more than qualified for. But he hadn't performed any jobs, and so he hadn't received any ratings or feedback.

Finally, someone was willing to take a chance on Isaac and they were satisfied with the work he completed. He received a favorable rating. "After that first 5-star rating, which is the most noticeable thing on my profile page, the jobs came easier," Isaac says. He has since received more favorable ratings and, he says, it is easier to get the jobs he wants. His success has been determined by his performance, yes, but also by the visible feedback he has received from others.

As a profile owner, you do not have a direct control over what is written about you. The features not controlled by you include referrals, ratings, and testimonials, as well as other, more creative implementations. A user's reputation is affected by how they relate to other people in the real world, and also by how they conduct themselves in an online network. It is therefore important to give honest and real testimonials. As you build your profile, request testimonials from trusted sources and remember their reputation impacts your own reputation. It is ideal to ask for these from someone who is active online; or digitally reputable, perhaps a manager or entrepreneur. Do not fake the testimonials and do not request them from friends who are fraudulently pretending to be someone they are not.

Some social networking sites include a place for an endorsement or feedback. These are an explicit part of the reputation system of social business sites. Few, but not many, sites require the user to approve the testimonial that is written about them before it is published. Many networking sites employ a system that allows users to rate each other, via scoring and commentary, adding positively or negatively to the user's reputation. These rating systems create a trust mechanism for all users.

The reputation system employed by oDesk, or similar sites like vWorker or Elance, are examples of ways that networks rely on transactions that are completed successfully or unsuccessfully to help determine the reliability of its users. Because of these systems, people are thought to act honorably or suffer financial consequences.

Your Voice From Two Perspectives

Your style imbues your message and your online presence with originality, competence, and professionalism, and thus, your presence is heavily weighted on the words, phrases, and images you use. To help with your selection, there are two ways to look at it:

- What people can see and interpret from your profile and presence.
- What the web or, more specifically, search engines see and interpret of your profile and presence.

From the Eyes of a Person

You will complete some heavy work in the next chapter in regard to selecting keywords to help develop your profile. Using the most relevant words to your industry today is a key to positioning yourself for success. The answer is in folklore and **folksonomies**.

Folklore is an important part of science and technology because it consists of idiosyncratic information about the ways in which equipment, processes, or technology really work, as well as the tricks necessary to generate good results. You won't read about it in journal articles or manuals, and it is typically conveyed by word of mouth. More recently, it has been applied to social media and SBS through tagging or, more broadly, through folksonomies. Wikipedia describes folksonomies as the classification system for creatively managing and organizing tags and content. The terminology may be new to you; the usage, however, is not. Think about how many acronyms you have memorized or buzzwords you have used in a business exchange or presentation this week. How about insider terms for an expertise or a methodology? We use these to signify that we know something, that we have access to that knowledge, which therefore we have chosen to use and apply. In addition, it's received by some readers as a signal of how well-versed you are in your area of specialty. Folksonomies are very collaborative and social in nature.

Currently, folksonomies are everywhere and can be picked up on a phone call with a peer or customer, during a conversation at work, or searching for information online. When using folksonomies and folklore, people are likely to consider you 'friendly', someone familiar, or relatable. We have to decide on an individual basis whether we will incorporate certain folksonomies. There are tools to help make this decision, most notably Google Alerts. Google Alerts allows you to automate the monitoring of certain terms and phrases according to three categories: news, blogs, and web. As the word "alert" signifies, Google searches for pre-set alert words or phrases and sends an email to the alert's creator when these are found. This is a near real-time system that allows a vigilant social business professional to stay current with the most recent developments. These can include your name, industry, peer, products and services, or anything else you can think of that's relevant to your profession.

There are some basic guidelines that will help you get the most from this free service.

1. **Start with no more than 2 or 3 alerts total**. It is tempting to create an alert for anything that interest you, but experience has

shown that they will quickly become unmanageable. The value lies in the real-time nature of the alerts, so it is more important to create a few that matter to you and read them regularly.

2. **Select keywords that are closely related to your industry or area of expertise.** This is critical because word association (for example, related words or synonyms) is a key component of search engine optimization. It also plays into other types of searches, like meta-data (tags) and semantic. These associated words, when discovered, should also be incorporated into your profile in order to maximize the profile's effectiveness.

3. **Try to capture the sources (URLs) from which the most reliable information comes.** Remember, many companies and people use keywords to drive traffic to a generic site to sell ads, and their information most often is a duplicate or without context (for example, no author or background information)– meaning it is less valued. You can verify the sources (URL) by going to Alexa.com and researching their traffic ranking. Basically if they are ranked on Alexa, then there is some indication that they are reliable.

4. **Within a few days or one week, depending on how often you get the alerts, notice the frequency by which a certain phrase or story is repeated by different sources.** This should give you an indication of what is trendy right now. Of course, you don't want to use trends or fads on your profile, but this is a great way to keep you in fashion, information fashion that is.

5. **Learn to use and adapt your phrases so that your alerts get more specific and useful.** This means you need to understand how to eliminate results from unreliable URLs. You'll also want to eliminate those that contain certain phrases that make the term related to a different topic area or those are from only a

certain type of domain extension (for example, .org, .edu, .com). You should wait until you can use these advance search features to start to grow the amount of Google Alerts you have. As each phrase gets more concise and useful, you can increase the number of alerts because it should report less and, therefore, allow you to manage more alerts.

From the Eyes of a Search Engine

How search engines see your presence is really an extension of how people search for you. At its essence, this requires you to understand what phrases people will use to find you and whom you are competing with in order to rise up to the top of the search results.

Search engine optimization (SEO) works regardless of whether you are using Google, the search engine within LinkedIN or any other private or gated professional networking website. Search engine optimization is a practice that focuses on keyword selection and usage; it determines ranking. This is a rich subject area with a wide variety of tactics, methodologies, and schools of thought.[3] One relevant premise from the SEO world is relativity. For example, if a word is too popular, you are going to have to compete with a variety of companies and marketers who have legions of SEO experts and extensive resources to compete with. Most likely, you will lose. On the flip side, the more popular a word is, and the frequency of its association with your name, the better your overall results will be with selected words. This is one of the reasons SEO experts advocate putting your profile on many different popular networks, like Google Me and LinkedIN, because search engines love these popular, heavily trafficked networks, and the association alone ensures that your ranking within a search engine will most likely be higher, or at a minimum, will outrank someone who is not so focused on the Me Paradox or have read this book.

As you become better at the art of ranking words, you will be ready to develop a niche strategy, if you choose. This is optimal because you improve your chances of appearing near the top of searches tenfold due to the niche nature of the audience. The thinking here is that it is better to have more of less than a lot of nothing. The combination of your online profile, your profession, the activities you do online, and your goals will define how successful you are with your online reputation, and thus SEO is important, but it's not the end all, be all for your online reputation strategy.

Google PageRank Algorithm,[4] although secret to most of the world, works on the premise that the more links to your site, profile or blog, the more popular, or relevant, you are. Or as Google puts it, "each link from site A to a page on site B adds to site B's PageRank." Although this is not perfect, it is fairly effective. Another consideration is the more popular your links are, the better. Why? Because again, the more people looking at a site that mentions you or links to you, the more popular the algorithm thinks you are and thus, ranks you accordingly. This means you want to put your profile in several public listing domains such as LinkedIN, ZoomInfo, and Plaxo, just to name a few. But, and here is a big BUT, if you have great content associated to you already–let's say an award, publication, or professional contributions that made it online, it makes sense to only list in one profile directory (preferably the most popular one) and link to those high-ranking search results. The best practice is to not dilute yourself by putting your profile in multiple popular directories, and push the accreditation and reputation-building attributes to the back pages.

Finally, if possible, make sure the links are bi-directional. If you link to your blog or somehow link your company's webpage to your online profile, it will improve your ranking. It is important to capitalize on synergies of highly trafficked websites and websites that contain information about you. Also, linking to images and other rich media can be effective. Search engines today are programmed to link and return a variety of search results types, and thus, having some sort of link may allow you to increase your online profile ranking. Even when you struggle to compete with a plaintext webpage in your particular expertise or industry, you may succeed overall using a linkage to rich media as it segments you into a different search result category.

You should now understand the importance of your online presence and how to start thinking about it in terms of your online reputation. But understanding and building are two different things. The next chapter will help you physically build your presence using hands-on strategies to assess your goals, assess your profile, and to create documents that will help you construct your online reputation.

~chapter four~
Building an Online Presence

B uilding an online presence requires work; it's a construction. You don't have to wear a hard hat or swing a hammer, but this work is still tiring and time-consuming. You will need to think, to write, and to analyze things on multiple levels. You may even want to keep a pen and paper handy as you read on. As mentioned, and keeping the Me Paradox in mind, this work that sometimes seems tedious can really pay off later when it comes to your online presence.

Just like with any construction, it's logical to think of starting with the foundation when building your online presence. This foundation includes your goals, which help you establish where your profile will be seen, who will be seeing it, and for what reasons.

- Consider your short-term and long-term goals
- Categorize and prioritize these goals
- Find your profile a home

Understanding your goals is the first step. Like any probable strategy, directive or business case, we need a charter that helps us make decisions as we go along, and to keep us consistent. Maybe you want to land an interview, career advancement, attract a client, find a mentor, or something else entirely. Jot down some ideas, keeping in mind that your goals should account for your resources, skills, the industry you are in, and your competition within that industry.

Goal Assessment

There are three (3) high-level goals that should help you think through some of your personal initiatives.

Goal 1: To Learn

Before you can set precise goals you need to learn about your industry. Ask yourself the following questions.

- Who are the leaders in your field?
- What are these leaders talking about (i.e. the latest trends in your industry)?
- What are the problems that need to be solved?
- What is the next area to learn?

Realize that learning comes from participation. The reservoir of knowledge created by the confederations of self-designated experts and volunteers can often exceed the sum of the parts. Call it the wisdom of the crowd or collective intelligence, but a group of your peers will have incredible amounts of information that the Internet, at this time, has too much of.

Think about this vast sea of information and ask yourself:

- What is relevant?
- What is the contribution that makes YOU more valuable?
- Would you trust the advice from a stranger you found in a search, or would you prefer to listen to advice from someone with an established reputation?

Goal 2: Be Proactive

Companies are adopting SBS for internal purposes. Think about how you will succeed when it truly starts to count. Flying under the radar, or non-disclosure of **tacit knowledge**, is no longer a viable strategy to ensure job security or a competitive edge. As an increasing number of companies are adopting and deploying internal social networks, getting used to this medium is critical and at this point, waiting is not an option.

Moreover, companies are transitioning to telecommuting at an increasing rate. Forrester[1] reports escalating numbers as more tools and processes are developed to subcontract over the Internet, and to do it effectively and efficiently. By learning about SBS now, you are not only being defensive, but you are also being aggressive. This is where you gain security, not only in your job, but also in your career.

Goal 3: Networking for Your Career

Douglas Fowler from the New Hampshire Business Review states that "more job leads are developed and discovered through networking than any other method— between 40 and 70 percent of jobs are found and filled through networking." The networks create opportunities for you to find your next job or, alternatively, provide you with enough visibility to attract a business opportunity. We are now in the Gig Economy.[2] We do a host of different types of work to make ends meet. Having just one job or staying in one narrow field is becoming uncommon. You might be collaborating with others on some projects and working alone on others. These may vary and could include writing a paper or book, being involved in an entrepreneur group, participating in an association, etc. One focus might be highly centered on subject matter expertise where others will be focused on networks and role-based efforts.

Reality Check for Your Goals

Despite the nature of your goals, consider your resources and be realistic. For instance, if a goal requires 20 hours per week you will need the time or money that would allow you to dedicate 20 hours per week toward that goal. We need to take stock of who we know and who they know, and what we have available to us in terms of time and money. And, because most of us have limited resources available to us, we need to build an economy that will help us best utilize these resources.

Profile Assessment

With our goals in mind, we will start thinking about creating a profile, but not without some advanced preparation. Here are some exercises that will help you determine your direction and create your profile strategically. You might want to grab a pen and paper for these next few exercises, but leave your resume out of sight for the moment:

- Consider what it would take to achieve your short- and long-term goals. Now create two categories:
  - the goals you are sure about
  - the goals you hope to achieve if all the stars align
- In one or two sentences, summarize where you are in your career. This can also be thought of as a mission statement about who you are. Remember to keep it brief, and no cheating with the resume. This description should be centered on discovering *who* you are. Even if you think you know yourself and the exercise sounds silly to you, humor me. Later, you'll understand the reason for it.
  - Who am I? Where am I going in my career?
- Begin to build your inventory of skills (still no cheating with the resume). When thinking about your skills, consider the current economic environment and industry fundamentals, which should give your skills a slight twist.
- Brainstorm a list of skills and separate them into the following categories:
  - Specialized skills for the industry
  - Skills useful in this current economic environment

- Now, take out your resume and use that to list your skills from top to bottom with the most marketable at the top. Do not worry about using keywords, buzzwords, or the words your competitors use. No need to be concerned with industry phrases at this point either.
  - o Skills per resume
  - o most marketable → least marketable

Your Skills Inventory

This inventory of skills will be helpful as we get into the next sections and work toward how we can best articulate ourselves for our audiences, and, in many cases, in ways that are advantageous to the mechanisms by which search engines find us.

Now, take some time to think about your industry and try to characterize what it takes to be successful. The better we understand the industry we are in or the people we are competing against, the better we will do. Our friend, Brad, is a perfect example. Brad left the technology industry to go into construction, thinking there were too many smart people in technology. His logic revolved around a thought that he could do better in an industry where the number of competitors with an advanced degree was significantly smaller. What he failed to realize was two-fold:

(1) It takes a lot more resources to gain any traction in construction than in his previous industry. Rather than $1,000 laptop with pre-installed software, he was looking at renting equipment or buying materials that cost tens of thousands of dollars.

(2) The skills he needed to be successful in his new industry were vastly different from those he needed to be successful in the one he left. Being a natural introvert, Brad didn't do so well in an industry where he needed to network the old-fashioned way.

Ultimately, Brad achieved nominal success, but admitted that with the same amount of effort and tenacity in the technology industry, he most likely would have bested what he achieved in construction. Failing to recognize what your industry composition is and how to best use what you have at your disposal has more of an impact than most would understand.

Of course, factors are going to change from industry to industry, but here are a few questions you can ask yourself to help you brainstorm about the current trends in your own industry so you don't make the same mistake as Brad:

- Describe the current economic trend (e.g. boom or bust):
- What are the associations or governing bodies/groups specific to your industry?
- Who are the thought leaders in the industry?
- Which buzzwords are used throughout the industry?
- Who are the big players and companies in your industry?
- Where do you stand in the industry according to years of experience (e.g. a first year or veteran)?
- Who is your competition?

Study Yourself; Study Your Competitors

If you establish your foundation with proper due diligence, do the research, and then act, your chances of success are so much better. There are various strategies, but all of them start with knowing and recognizing who you're up against and how you will exceed industry expectations.

This may be a challenge. Most people do not understand the perception they create online. Psychologist Sam Gosling of the University of Texas, Austin, has found that while profiles on social networking sites like Facebook present a generally accurate portrait of their owners, this portrait is often at odds with the impression the owners think they are putting across. According to Gosling, people are not good at judging the impression they make on others online.

By researching your peers and better understanding the world around you, you are in a better position to deliver an effective and authentic signal underpinned by your profile. Thus, a study of your competitors will help you understand the do's and don'ts of presenting yourself online:

1. **Start by searching for a peer profile online, perhaps of someone in your industry.**
    a. Check to see if they have a blog, or whether or not they comment regularly on other industry sites or blogs.
2. **Now, look around for their profile.**
    a. Where does it live?
    b. Does it have more than one home?
3. **What do you notice about their online activities?**
    a. Notice what is written about them and compare that to what you know about them in reality.
    b. Determine whether there is a vast difference between who you know them to be and how they portray themselves online.

What your online profile says about you may not take into consideration what occurs in face-to-face or real-world interactions. Indeed, you can learn a lot by people who are already out there because many of them have a battle-tested strategy. Comparing their tactics to your goals will help you define your own approach.

Your Unique Identifier

Now that you've considered your goals and other factors that shape your filters, let's talk about some of the finer details of crafting that presence. The first consideration is your name. It is critical to know where you stand. Go to a few popular search engines and type in your name, and then search for your name combined with a few keywords. These can be previous companies, titles, and skills. Also, try variant spellings of your name. What type of results do you get? There are two basic scenarios to consider: *common names* and *unique names*.

Common names: How many Mike Smiths are there in the world? If you fall in the category of having a common name, your main concern will be differentiating yourself. You can use a middle name, or your middle initial; or choose a different spelling of your name. Possibly the best way to differentiate yourself is to associate a professional title, degree, or distinguishing characteristic with your name; if you choose this tactic, stay consistent with it in all of your online activity. After you've examined the ways in which your competition tries to differentiate themselves, think about how someone might try to find you, specifically, among all the Mike Smiths in the world, then play to your strengths in that area, perhaps by listing your association with a known place, school, or company.

Unique names like Suzy Schletteranski have a very different problem than Mike Smith. Once someone learns to spell her last name (possibly no small task), she and her family will be easy to find on the World Wide Web. If Ms. Schletteranski only uses the Internet for professional purposes, then she has little to worry about; but if she has a Facebook profile to stay in touch with friends and family, she can end up inadvertently revealing far too much, simply because she's not buried in the millions of pages of search results as would occur with the last name Smith. Even if nothing problematic is on her Facebook page, it can dilute her cumulative message to the point where she appears unprofessional to a potential interviewer.

If Suzy wants to differentiate her personal presence from her professional one, she may try using just Suzy S. or a family nickname. Be careful, though: even a few slips of using your professional identifiers can make the effort worthless—or worse yet, embarrassing. There are some situations where you may have gone by a nickname, say as a researcher in grad school, but you used your formal name at your first professional job where you worked with a different audience. There might be somewhat of a struggle in trying to quantify which name to start developing your presence with, since both have credible references. At this point, it may be appropriate to understand your Google Quotient. Google Quotient is a term that was popularized by William Arruda and Kirsten Dixon. Basically, these two researchers attempt to quantify what your name results in when searched using Google's search engine—you can see how they quantify your name at careerdistinction.com/onlineid. This tool could help you compute which name has the most value.

This leads me to wonder about your own domain (i.e. www.yourname.com). As a preservation strategy, and in an effort to protect your future endeavors, if you can get it, you will want to grab your name's domain and any variations used for a potential blog or future website. It typically only costs a couple of dollars and less than $10-per year to maintain—a nominal expense when compared to the opportunity it can create. Once people catch on, it might be more expensive and even impossible to get, so grab it now and hold onto it for later.

BEST PRACTICE REVIEW

Do not take on another spelling of your name or a nickname just to avoid a negative criticism or feedback. Experts recommend contacting the website administrator of the website that hosts the negative commentary, and ask them to remove it or allow a rebuttal. In addition, there are companies like ReputationDefender.com that, for a fee, will do some of that leg work for you. Trackur.com is another great place to start and find your web mentions.

It is important to actively manage the first 3 to 5 pages as you periodically Google your name. These few pages are the most crucial as most searches do not go beyond the first 3 pages of a search engine result. Ideally, this management would consist of actively publishing, claiming automated pages about you, and contacting owners or publishers talking about you and your industry, especially those displaying a negative tone or sentiment.

The important takeaway is transparency. Attempts at purely trying to hide or avoid negative comments is considered sneaky and if discovered, highly damaging. The time has come where having a blemish and dealing with it speaks volumes about your character, and if this is your situation, wear it as a badge of honor as opposed to risking being discovered and flagged as someone with compromised ethics.

At the very least, have an explanation prepared about why the negative event occurred and be able to describe in detail what you have done to remedy that situation. Transparency, at the end of the day, will win over mistakes and errors in judgment.

A subjective tactic that is garnering some press is to bury your negative comment by actively publishing content. Be aware that if the activity veers toward SPAM and SPLOG, this gray area could be considered unethical. To a certain extent, for search engine optimization tactics to be effective, they necessitate that the content be rich in quality. This is so the content's popularity (including those who link to it) will help to increase the ranking by bubbling the content up to the first pages of search engine results. The best strategy for a professional appearance in Google results is to take the

Long Tail approach, which, as you recall, will help you to continue to move forward in developing your online reputation. Through time and diligence, the negative comments eventually become outweighed by the positive and sheer volume of your presence.

Truth in Profiles

Some folks on purely social or dating websites tend to assume false identities, whether it's a contemporary pseudonym or a stylish but misleading photo. Be aware that this tactic does not work so well in the professional world. Identity theft is even more difficult to monitor as most networking sites are not able to identify who is legitimate and who is not. Not only should you be honest in your own representation, but you should also avoid someone you know is misrepresenting. Mature and professional networks have developed ways that the members cooperate to weed out **fakesters**, and it helps your own reputation to cooperate in that effort.

Even without outright falsehood, there are often temptations to insinuate or elaborate on our experiences. Don't be impulsive. Instead, take the time to vet what you are about to post about yourself. This is of paramount importance. Don't forget the general rule of thumb: 'when in doubt, leave it out'. If it is questionable or even marginally controversial, avoid it. Think of your post as a personal email you would write to introduce yourself to your company president. Read and reread the information, check it for accuracy, and even sleep on it to make sure that everything said is as intended.

Profile Framework

After thinking about goals, filters, and appropriate online protocols, you are now ready to begin crafting your online profile. To do this, I will start by giving you the tools you will need to build your profile framework. It might help to create an Excel or any type of spreadsheet, or just simply use your pen and paper to make columns. You can label this personalized online reputation information database as yourname_version# (see figure 4-1 and 4-2).

Online Reputation Exercise

Consider this profile framework as central intelligence where decisions about your progress are made. These include how to proceed, when to evolve, and how to evaluate yourself.

Figure 4-1

PROFILE FRAMEWORK

Name:
Industry:
Goal:
Profile Fields:

Biography (Elevator Pitch)
Objective/Overall
Expertise and relevant experience
Education
Employment History
Additional Information
Hobbies
Profile Image Small (125px X 75px)
Profile Image Large (400px X 400px)

Keywords:

Use the paper where you jotted down your goals earlier and create one column for short-term goals and another for your long-term goals.

If your list of goals includes more than ten, try to narrow it down to the ten (five short-term and five long-term) that are most important to you.

WORKSHEET #1 – DEFINING GOALS
- List those goals in the appropriate columns and order them by priority of personal importance.
- Create another column where you will list the audience (people or community) associated with each specific goal. This is a tougher question because within it is the notion that you already know who can help you achieve your career goals. Don't stress. Simply create the column and venture a guess. The later sections will help you define and evaluate your audience.

Figure 4-2

SKILLS DEFINTION WORKSHEET

	Skill	Relevancy	Popularity	Applicability
1				
2				
3				
4				
5				
6				
7				

WORKSHEET #2 – DEFINING SKILLS (see figure 4-2)
- Start a new page or spreadsheet labeled "skills." In Column 1, list your skills as words and short phrases. Think of them as

buzzwords in your field that are used at work or online. It could also be the terms used in articles you are reading or materials you are studying from. Another way to find particular words is to refer back to your peer's bio. What words are they using in their profiles? You are not going to use every word here necessarily. The objective is to simply list them and have them available for later.

- In Column 2, create a 'Relevancy Score'. The relevancy score will be placed in the scoring column and should rate how applicable this word is to describing you. This can be entered in terms of 1 for closely related (for example, expertise or something you're passionate about) and a 5 for loosely related or not all (for example, some experience or not interested in any longer). Once you have this list down, add a few more words by going to Google's *Synonym Lab* or Synonym website and run a few of the most generic and overly used but significant words through the system. Per the definition, is this term relevant to you? List it and then score it like the buzzwords.

- Now create a third column for the keyword's popularity score. First you will need to find the "Google Keyword Tool" at adwords.google.co.in/select/KeywordToolExternal and type in the most applicable words (where you gave a relevancy score of 1 or 2). The tool is critical as it shows how much volume a keyword generates in searches, which also helps when considering the competition. The heavily advertised word is also the most competitive, according to most search engine optimization theorists. The ideal keyword is the one with the most volume but the least competitive. Look at the columns and score the words as follows: 1= most volume, least competitive,

2=most volume and most competitive, 3=least volume and least competitive and finally, 4=least volume and most competitive.

- Now, add the two scores and evaluate the results. Sort them with lowest total first and highest total last. How did they change?

- In column 4, you will create a space for the applicability test, which is your final and most important indicator. Go to the people and communities column of your goals sheet and type the names with the most relevant (relevancy score 1 or 2) and popular (popularity score 1 or 2, and 3 if you were not able to find many 1's) keywords into the Google search engine. Try multiple combinations. Examine and analyze the types of results you get. If the first page is relevant (nearly all are good sources and have coherent content that contains both the buzzword and the people/communities), then you will put a check in the 4th column. This does not have to be exact; just follow your gut instinct. The idea is you will use all the checkmarks and ignore the words and phrases that are blank.

It's All Semantics

Essentially, we want to associate the words that you are using with the words others in your industry are using and place these in our profile. We mapped our relevancy and the popularity with the usage, which should help us determine which words are critical. This will also work for your traditional resume as many of the resume search programs used by human resource departments operate under the same premise.

Next, we want to list our industry segments and characteristics. Don't forget to have three columns available with each keyword so that we may score it, add a comment to it, and test its applicability.

This becomes a key filtering factor in the networks you will participate in and the peers and potential business contacts you will make.

Some example of characteristics include whether or not your industry is stable, growing, or declining. We also need to evaluate the associations and thought leaders, and describe them with as many keywords as possible. The main idea here is to use the keywords to describe your industry, giving you insight into it, as demonstrated by the volume or signs of growth or decline.

The Details Matter

Using your words list and scores again, start to think about which of these words can be honestly incorporated into your business profile. Be pragmatic and sincere with yourself. Have realistic goals, but think of your business profile as a slab of stone you will build your foundation on. You want it to be sound and stable; something that will last. The framework of varying profile fields exists so you do not have to recreate your profile for every network you join.

To prepare yourself, use the Profile Framework for background information, but open a new worksheet to begin developing your professional profile. You will want to use specific fields, but realize these are not all-inclusive. Think of it as a set of basic guidelines that can be replicated and used repeatedly.

Your **objective** or **overview** column is a suitable place to insert the essentials of the message or impression you're trying to communicate. A one- or two-sentence tagline is all you will need. It should incorporate keywords or buzz terms relevant to your profession. You will want to put your elevator pitch–for example, your highly streamlined summary of who you are and what you do–in the **Background** or **Biography** column. Just keep in mind that you will have about 5-10 seconds to catch the reader's attention. The more meaningful your summary is, the more your readers will stay engaged and will want to continue reading.

For your **education** column, unless you went to an Ivy League school or graduated summa cum laude, stick to the basics. The same rules apply when describing your **skills** or **expertise**. You want to place the focus only on the phrases and words that differentiate you from your competition. This is the place for buzzwords and key search terms; you also have to be willing to narrow down your listing to what you're really best at. Like the old cliché, a 'jack-of-all-trades' often comes across as a master of none. Furthermore, it won't help an employer find you and it won't land you that dream job.

In your **employment history**, convey not only what you do, but what the job or career you are going after looks, acts, and feels like. Envision what a future employer will want to see in you as a candidate, then briefly describe the company's mission and how you helped contribute to it. Stay succinct, even if you are at the peak of a full career. And, I can't stress enough that you should not hesitate to use your peers for comparison; this helps ensure that you're describing yourself in language that's appropriate for the industry.

It's crucial to have a couple of different photos available to use as part of your profile: one ultra-conservative, another taken in a more casual setting. Personal images allow people to relate to you, even when communicating with you virtually. They are also a highly memorable feature that can distinguish you from your competition.

For your **additional information**, you might include special certifications, training, permits, security clearance, or the like. In this section, it helps to round out your profile here with a few key interests. Here you might add websites that showcase your abilities or passions. For instance, maybe you belong to a trade association or an interest group; you can help others find you by naming those groups and linking to them. If you're an award winner, recognized by peers, customers, or employers, add prestige without bragging by listing them here.

Your **hobbies** also communicate important information about you: blogging is an important skill for a communications person; extreme sports show a competitive instinct that could be valuable in a marketing or sales job. Your particular abilities and interests, the personal values you bring to your professional performance, and even a note of humor and passion, all help your network understand who you are.

It's important to include an **introduction paragraph** about you. This is a quick bio that helps to describe you and can be offered or requested for various reasons, including speaking engagements, collaboration projects, and other activities you will eventually get involved in. Recruiters and placement agencies also like these bios as it's something they can add to your resume as they represent you. Keep this bio short and succinct–an introduction longer than 4 to 5 sentences is not necessary. It basically needs to showcase who are you from a professional perspective (e.g. hard-working, ex-CEO of Exxon, 20-year veteran), your accomplishments and then your skills, in that order.

Proceed With Caution

Some notes to keep in mind:

- Avoid stating personal views about other people or companies, especially if they are negative.
- Be careful with posting your views on politics, religion, and other contentious issues. Even those who don't agree with your position on these often-controversial topics may present business opportunities, and you don't want to miss out on these

simply because you don't vote the same way or attend the same church.

- Finally, never assume even in a private network, that your information is not accessible. There is always someone out there with the skills to get to it if they really want to.

The Weight of Your Words

New media has created alternative ways to communicate online. But for business and professional purposes, online communication remains fundamentally based on your ability and command of the language. When you assess your online communication skills, think about the specific words you use to carry a sentence. It goes far deeper than your ability to write a grammatically correct sentence. As I've mentioned, face-to-face communication is exponentially more expressive. No amount of emoticons can compare with facial expressions and body language because these go on ad infinitum. There are certain words businesspeople should know and use, and others that they should avoid. How familiar are you with the appropriate language in your industry? How do you expand your repertoire of terms and phrases? Your non-verbal activity gives a few online cues about you. For instance, a history of sites visited can be informative. An extensive vocabulary is not as important as understanding the connotations and implications of a word and its related expressions.

This kind of attention to nuance develops your individual voice as an online writer. These are the communication skills of tonality: perfecting the tone of your writing, which, more than anything else, will differentiate you from the pack. Your voice can be distinguished by both what you express and how you express it; how you share your points of view and how you cultivate meaningful dialogue with others. Voice is a huge part of our reputations. In a world based on relationships and communication, how you talk to others is part of who you are.

Think about how you use your voice and the style in which you present yourself in face-to-face communication. You probably put a lot of effort into making sure that the signals you send, down to the words you choose and the pacing of your speech, is aligned with your actions. The same should be true of your voice during professional activities online, including publishing your bio, a press release, or even a blog or message board posting in a professional community. Writing clearly, persuasively, and with authority are the online equivalents of making sure that you don't stutter or rush your face-to-face speech. The big difference is that online, there's not the wealth of additional information nor is there the opportunity for the listener to ask you to repeat yourself. The subtle signals are even more important online due to the weight words bear.

Where the Rubber Meets the Road

You might have noticed how I went back and forth between using the terms online profile and online presence. Online presence is the compilation of multiple profiles and identity markers online. At the very basic level, your online profile is what you control. You build it, write it, post it, and update it; allows a user to communicate their personal and professional details to all other users within a network. Ultimately, your online profile is what you are according to what you say. Now your online reputation is your online presence and everything else about you. It is your composite online, and this is defined by what you write and what everyone else writes and how that all interacts with you and your contacts and content–even by mistake or accident.

In the following chapters we will get into the difference between topic-focused and relationship-focused networks. These networks have different strengths and weaknesses because the network is what you depend on to create trust, and that trust allows you to exchange social capital to get you closer to your goals. But first, we will explore what makes social business possible which is the key to choosing the right network.

~chapter five~

~chapter five~
Participation: The Cornerstone

Participation is at the heart of your life online. Like other parts of the Me Paradox, participation isn't about you. It puts you in touch with networks that create value and help you reach your ultimate goals. It is about exchanges, and those exchanges give you the opportunity to build and trade social capital. Understanding the difference between talking with the people you know well and networking with others to expand your opportunities is one of the more difficult parts of the Me Paradox. But it's not an impossible obstacle to overcome.

In order to build and create an online reputation, you will need to strategically decide how, when, and where to participate. This goes for every stage of your interaction with the social web, from establishing presence, through networking, to engaging. And, it becomes the basis for each and every exchange where you trade social capital to reach your intended goals. To understand how this works, we need to take a close look at participation and what it means.

The Essence of Taking Part

Participation takes many forms. If you think about it, shopping is participation–albeit the most passive form. Amazon's suggestions demonstrate how shopping gives the company knowledge that is used to inform other buyers, which, in turn, influences their purchase behavior. This has real impacts, especially in a marketplace like Amazon's, where others' opinions are very valuable because the actual products can't be handled. But the people who generated that information didn't do anything special to make the information more valuable. The system transformed their aggregated data into something useful to potential buyers.

Who Participates and How?

Until recently, when most users were seeking information on the Internet, they typically found what they were looking for and then stopped looking. No further interaction was needed. But social networking sites are much different. They are defined by interaction and participation. This is another example of the Me Paradox: When you understand how to relate to and interact with others in this new age of technology, you will reap tremendous benefits for yourself.

Nonetheless, people have a wide variety of reasons for not participating online. It's time consuming, it requires effort, it may lead to embarrassment in the future, and so on. Some of us simply don't see any need to participate. While this may have been true in the past decade, it is far from truth in today's society.

The *Social Network 1% Rule* (see figure 5-1) was created by Don Dodge and Bradley Horwitz, and it came about as a result of a study intended to understand the distribution of participation.

The rule, according to Dodge, states that generally, in a group of 100 people online, one will create content, nine will "interact" with it (commenting or adding to it) and the other 90 will just view it. But, everyone benefits from the activities of the group.

Figure 5-1

SOCIAL NETWORK 1% RULE

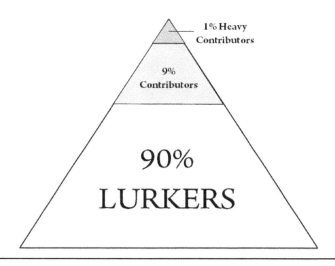

This is important contextual information to keep in mind when looking at sites like Wikipedia, as the rule seems to better describe sites with no monetary incentive for the people using them. Internal or workplace networks have different participation distributions with a much greater proportion of serious and minor active participants. No one knows exactly how many of us participate, largely because participation is difficult to define. Participation figures change constantly, and participation rates are climbing for certain social networking sites and the social web as a whole.

At the Heart of Social Networking: Emotions

Websites that are devoted to the business world have a different distribution, but there too, not everyone participates equally. There is more to be gained in a professional setting–contacts, for instance, as well as business opportunities. Some of us will be more active than others. The overall tendency has been for an increasing number of people to be more active. As technologies continue to develop and become more widespread, we are creating and saving much more information than we ever have. The sharing and participating mentality is becoming prevalent in modern day society, but it's not all-pervasive. Not yet.

Researchers are looking for answers. In one study, they sought to determine why some people lurk and others participate more actively. They discovered, among other things, that we use social media to satisfy social and emotional needs. The results of a 2008 study[1] demonstrated that the level of verbal and affective intimacy in a given network positively impacted posting frequency. In other words, people expected gratification in the form of intimacy, and when they received it, their participation increased. So it just stands to reason that participation in social networks is determined by much more than the information flow. It's based on the human aspect of emotional interaction.

The pitfall associated with this tendency is that a negative reinforcement cycle is also possible. Those who lurk on social networking sites may do so because they tend to believe their social and emotional needs will not be met if they participate. This belief can become self-fulfilling. If you post and no one responds, you may be so put off that you no longer want to post. This potential problem is avoided by carefully crafting your posts, avoiding impulsive and random posts, especially when they are meant to hone in on others' conversations. After all, if you were in a face-to-face situation you wouldn't jump into a stranger's conversation. That's why it's important to decide which networks you want to contribute to ahead of time. This decision is the first step in choosing the types of information you want to share. Make the effort to choose your networks and choose the times and places to participate, and you'll benefit by having your emotional and social needs met.

Thinking Globally

You may be thinking, why go to all this effort just for the emotional benefits? But try to think of things in a more universal manner. Take yourself out of your own mindset and put yourself in the mind of the global economy: a place where ideas can be shared and products can be bought and sold without leaving your home or office.

A comment on an Amazon product or a do-it-yourself tip on eHow might help others but, you may think, how can that benefit me? Most of us tend to put in a fairly low amount of effort for solely altruistic reasons. Businesses are even less likely to expend time and resources for altruistic postings, unless they are charities or non-profits. Businesses act online for the same reasons they do any kind of public relations: because it will benefit them in the long term. By imagining and understanding the long-term benefits of these gestures is something businesses and many individuals have not completely grasped just yet.

To conquer involves re-imagining your role in a larger social network. This mindset helps you understand how actively participating in social networks for the benefit of others will payoff for you. It will satisfy your emotional needs as well as your career goals. It is the Me Paradox in action.

Become a Source of Wisdom

The biggest benefit of these network interactions is much more than just the exchange of information, or even the sense of community that meets our emotional needs. It's wisdom. Information is just data, just a mass of facts that may or may not mean anything to a particular person. When something has been learned, it becomes knowledge, but knowledge isn't just information that has been memorized (see figure 5-2), it's a complex social process that allows you to understand how to integrate information and act on it.

Figure 5-2

DATA EMERGENCE CHART

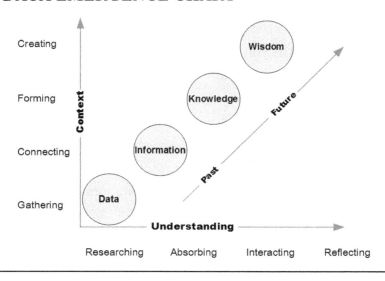

Wisdom is the result of putting that knowledge into practice, gaining from its experiences. Both knowledge and wisdom are context-dependent: what you know and how you know it depend upon the circumstances of your learning, including who taught you and how they taught you. Wisdom is doubly dependent upon both the teaching of knowledge and the self-teaching that emerges from experience. John Naisbitt said it best when he noted that we are, "drowning in information and starving for knowledge." That's true because 90 percent of people are "lurkers," according to *The Social Network 1%*

Rule. Yet we're also emerging and evolving and with this, we are beginning to realize how much we hunger for knowledge and wisdom, not just information. To get knowledge and wisdom, we need to get out of the social network "lurker" category; we need to be active participants.

Information Does Not Equal Knowledge

Having information is valuable. But without the context, it's less valuable. John Seely Brown, the chief information scientist at Xerox Corporation, is an authority on the social nature of information. He has published several papers and a popular book, *The Social Life of Information*,[2] where he argues that we need to look beyond the myth of information as being valuable by itself and examine the people who actively engage and diffuse it. Knowing the origin makes information more valuable. For example, you might not be as interested in Brown's argument if you didn't know that it came from an authoritative source.

The perceived value of information is also dependent upon the context of the person examining it. Information about a recent discovery of fossil fish jawbones from millions of years ago might not be valuable to the average person but, for a scientist who specializes in that area, it might be just the right piece of information to support or undermine an important theory. The perceived value of the information also depends on how easy it is to find the information. If ten people send you a link to the same front-page news article, none of them alone is very valuable. But a nugget unearthed and passed on at the right time and place can turn out to be gold (for example, a memo about a pending tech IPO).

The process of turning raw data into information and then into useful knowledge, or even wisdom, is becoming harder and harder for an individual to accomplish alone. According to the research firm IDC in 2008, the world created and copied 161 exabytes (an exabyte is one quintillion bytes or a billion gigabytes) of digital information. It was noted in that same report that they expect the number to grow six-fold to 988 exabytes by 2010. With sites like Wikipedia and Twitter, SPAM, blogs, and a flood of copycats posing as creators, we have increasing volumes of information that threaten to overwhelm our ability to transform it into knowledge. This is why it's essential for us to use networks to accomplish these tasks. Professionals must work together to collect, analyze, synthesize, and disseminate information throughout the work process. Even activities like information seeking are becoming collaborative efforts that take place through networks. These networks are the places where exchanges take place. And these exchanges provide everything from information to wisdom, and the process of the exchange itself creates more knowledge and more wisdom. So, in essence, your active participation in social business does pay off–you just have to find the right place to participate.

BEST PRACTICE REVIEW

Two social scientists[3] who have been observing the ways individuals in organizations use computer-mediated communications or CMC have written a book titled, *Connections: New Ways of Working in the Networked World* in which they point out that: This kind of informal lore exchange is a key part of every organization: "Does anybody know . . . " is a common phrase in organization–typically heard in informal encounters in office hallways, before meetings begin, at the water cooler, in lunchrooms, and on email. In the terms of the general information procedure, one person asks a search question that may be vague or ambiguous. Usually the asker is seeking a piece of information, not easily found in official documents. The audience for such questions usually knows the asker and is sympathetic or at least tolerant because the behavior is conventional, the questions are not onerous, and answerers themselves may one day need to ask a question.

In the conventional world, if the asker's contact cannot provide an answer, the asker is stymied. But with electronic communication, the asker has access to a broader pool of information sources. An oceanographer broadcasts a message to an online network of oceanographers: "Is it safe and reasonable to clamp equipment onto a particular type of insulating wire?" The official instructions said, "Do not clamp." Immediately, the sender received several responses from other oceanographers saying, "Yes, we do it all the time, but you have to use the following type of clamp." The oceanographer did not know the people who responded and would never have encountered them in a face-to-face setting, but through digital communication, he got much more than just the information or knowledge he might get from reading a manual or interacting with others around his office. He received wisdom, learned through experience, as a direct benefit of others engaging in that network. This information could have come from across continents rather than from just across the hall at the office.

Wisdom, as an emergent property gained by applying patterns of knowledge to different situations, is scarce, and therefore very valuable. Participating in networks is a way to gain access to others' wisdom, and in the process, create more for yourself and everyone else. The reservoir of information, knowledge, and wisdom created by a group of experts and volunteers pooling their resources is usually greater than the sum of its parts. The added value is supplied by the people who participate–the information may be readily available, but the communication makes all the difference. Again, it comes down to exchanges, and exchanges mean relationships.

Making Social Business Accessible

Participation is labor, and value depends on how much you work and the kind of work you do. You are not creating value if you are lurking and only taking in material, even when you are doing the work of integrating what you read into your own knowledgebase. The key to the Me Paradox is transforming data into information or information into knowledge; sharing that experience is what creates the value that can be exchanged with others. Whether you get to participate in these exchanges and obtain value in return for contribution depends on two things: your *level of engagement* and your *relationships*.

Research has found that existing social relationships significantly affect the ways individuals choose information. People tend to be motivated to seek information from resources available within their initial social network because it is easily accessible, quickly retrieved, and contextually rich. Likewise, people seek help from members that they interact with on a regular basis because they have developed a trusting relationship, which allows them to expose their information needs or share innovative information. In short, research suggests that people tend to seek information from the sources that are most easily accessible and locally available rather than from the best possible source.

SNS vs. Online Communities

Creating accessibility to your own knowledge and value is an important ingredient to participating in social business or within your workplace. By participating and sharing knowledge, you are positively growing your reputation by turning yourself into a great source!

Before we get into the intricacies of social business, let's explore the concepts that make up social business software.

Social networks are groups who have a shared interest or commonality; they are generally small, dense, and relatively homogenous. Social networks enabled by Social Networking Sites (SNS)–a distinct term popularized by Danah Boyd and Nicole Ellison[4] and used to describe part of the evolving process of social developments online–are massive but all loosely connected to the whole.

As SNS' wild success sparks the interest of the business world–and the eventual adoption of–have initiated a comparison with online communities (the business world's incumbent social media). You see, knowledge sharing and collaboration are old concepts in the business world. Businesses have tried various technologies to enable social connections with online communities as the reigning champion.

The differences between the tightly-knit online communities and SNS are analyzed in three major ways:

First, by design, social networking sites are specifically geared to help people establish an online presence and build social networks. They are people-focused, not topic-focused, and they foster the development of new encounters and relationships, whereas many traditional online communities are designed to improve a participant's understanding of a topic, thus are more topic-focused.

Second, people in an SNS are organized by their network of relationships. Unlike the hierarchically developed abstract rating system you might find in topic-focused networks like Slashdot, the links between member profiles are more indicative of the many ways information is distributed. It is people- and relationship-focused. Each user defines his or her network egocentrically–the way he or she sees and experiences it. In the topic-focused community model, the user's position is based on several factors including user history, which is often measured in terms of number of posts and pre-existing status.

This design recognizes top participants, giving experts and moderators with well-established histories more control than newly-arrived participants.

Third, in the relationship-driven context of SNS, users must explicitly state their relationships with others. These relationships are more visible, direct, and interpersonal than relationships found in online communities. Connections come before content, so we assume that people will define their identities more authentically on an SNS as compared with other online communities as this helps to assure meaningful connections. Relationships within an SNS are facilitated by providing an increasing number of interactive tools for connection building. There are avatars for self presentation, buddy lists for managing connections, and micro-blogging for staying up-to-date; there is also content published in profiles, blogs, and photo galleries to build new connections.

Social Business Sites or Software

There are an increasing number of software platforms being created to combine the best of both SNS and online communities. In the world of networking and business, this is exciting news! We refer to these topic-driven networking communities as Social Business Sites (for external-facing networks) or Social Business Software (for internal-facing networks).[5] Modeled after online communities, SBS is transportable, meaning they could be in-house, as in employee only Intranet, or web-based and available to members outside an organization. They are usually privileged sites for a tight, effective loop of insight, problem identification, learning, and knowledge production. Originally, these professional communities were small, limiting the available knowledge, but when social networking concepts are combined with these knowledge-producing communities, the resulting network has the ability to grow further, wider, and become much more diverse. This creates synergies that fuel a knowledge explosion.

Companies that adopted SBS showed massive benefits according to Forrester's 2008 report, *Why Companies Adopt Social Software*, which indicated that collaboration translates into innovation. Stronger ties increase employee retention. And, businesses truly become relationship-centric. Businesses surveyed were also able to reduce expenses, because opportunity costs were incurred when knowledge was not infused or retained, relationships were not transparent, and all were limited by departments or geography.

One of the earlier predictions about the profound effect social business would have on our society was by Pierre Levy,[6] who suggested in 2001 that ". . . cyberspace refers less to the new media of information transmission than to original modes of creation and navigation within knowledge, and the social relations they bring about."

Levy contended we are shifting from commodity space, which is focused on the production and consumption of goods, to knowledge space, which depends on social interactions to create knowledge. In essence, Levy was saying that we cannot continue to develop knowledge without connecting with other people. Innovation and the current state of enterprise are on a crash course with inter-departmental and -organizational working cultures–cultures that emphasize relationships as their foundation of knowledge creation.

But here's the clincher. Knowledge creation–and the relationships that foster it–can't just happen on their own. Organizations are only beginning to understand how to harness the power and benefits of the many tools that have been created for social interaction and they are beginning to realize that the most powerful developments can occur when such tools are combined, namely SBS.

Community, Networking, and SBS Structure

As figure 5-3 shows, when you couple communities with social networking, you have SBS. This is at the heart of the social business movement.

In order to understand why SBS is different, consider these four properties: Purpose, Method, Governance, and Trust.

Figure 5-3

SBS STRUCTURE

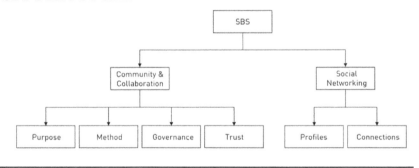

Community and Collaboration

As you ponder the words "community" and "collaboration," think about what it is that brings the people who live in your neighborhood together. Is it the close proximity? Now, what brings you together with another Ford truck owner? Commonalities form bonds, and this is what social business software designers spend their days concentrating on. These common attributes are a key ingredient to developing social business relationships.

A majority of traditional online forums or communities are built to improve one's understanding on any particular topic. This concept evolves as we participate and interact with other members within SBS.

Purpose

In order to have a community, there must be a common purpose. This sense of community is evident in social and business networks, even blogs, and other Web 2.0 tools. According to Harvard Business School Professor Mikolaj Jan Piskorski, "…online social networks are most useful when they address real failures in the operation of offline networks."

Use these 7 characteristics to help you brainstorm and interpret the purpose of the network you are considering:

1. Is it **magnetic**? In other words, what is it about this network that makes you feel passionate about it?
2. Is it **aligned** with what you want to accomplish, and do the benefits match what is stated or conveyed?
3. Is **value** stated, and if so, is the **value proposition** clear and is it low risk?
4. Is it **properly scoped**, or random and inconsistent?
5. Does it **facilitate evolution**? In other words, are people getting smarter and more connected by being a part of it?
6. Is the progress **measurable**?
7. Is the network **community-driven**, controlled by the members and not by the host? Some guidance is ok, but excessive governance can be a constraint.

Method

A method discussion begins, quite naturally, with a dialogue about features and functions. We need to know which mode the network operates in. There are some networks that prefer real-time communications. These include meetup (or face-to-face) groups and instant messaging (IM) centralized networks. Others are supported by conversation hubs known as blogs, wikis, and discussion forums, which involve many-to-many communication, collaborative content creation, Q&A, and, of course, all of these are asynchronously engaged: there is a lag between exchanges (see **BEST PRACTICE REVIEW** for more on discussion forums, wikis, and blogs).

Some of the tools used here are independent of SBS and others are incorporated into them. The blending of these conversational styles, which combine informal user interactions, information persistence, and information organization, make it possible to support a wide range of collaboration and communication scenarios.

At its simplest:

- **Discussion forums** are pure conversational tools
- **Blogs** involve personal perspective publishing
- **Wikis** are mainly personal- or group-information repositories

Given the difference between the three, it remains important to match the right tools to the collaboration style underlying any given business activity. For instance, a discussion forum is not the most efficient tool to use for a mentorship or a research network where the exchange is conversational and dynamic. In this type of forum, there are few controls over topic creation and development and therefore, a wiki may be more appropriate.

BEST PRACTICE REVIEW

Discussion forums are one way to communicate online. They are bottom heavy, meaning often important and useful information is posted near the bottom and the user has no control over the initial topic's development:

There is an upside to discussion forums:

- They are particularly useful for discussing new or controversial topics.
- The question and answer structure is good for developing teamwork.
- They are helpful when informally transferring knowledge, as in technical support or customer service.

On the downside, discussion forums:

- typically lack ways to organize or synthesize conversations.
- are not suitable as general-knowledge repositories.

Take for instance Wikipedia; this site would not do well as a discussion forum because the information is confused by the amount of participation and tracking from various information sources.

Contrarily, blogs are top heavy and supported by a broadcast format. The linking mechanisms, such as **blogrolls**, trackbacks, RSS, or just static links between blogs and other sources of information, act as the community and collaboration layer that sits on top of the main organizational mechanism. Until now, this type of communication took place over email or a flyer posting in the break room. If you look at a blog like a conversation hub, the original post is where the conversation spawns and develops. Blogs are mechanisms that control the development of a conversation more than any of the other tools listed.

In a discussion forum, a topic might start by discussing environmental devastation caused by the oil spill in the Gulf off Louisiana and wind up as a talk about the politicians who overwhelmingly supported offshore drilling in the United States.

You can pretty much spill your guts in a blog. Smart CEOs will use blogs but will steer clear of discussion forums and wikis. They use blogs to communicate with their customers and employees, because it sets the tone and is viewed as more of a broadcast, not a panel.

Take, for example, CEO of Marriott Hotels Bill Marriott, who regularly blogs to his customers about the quality of his hotel rooms, the executive decisions he has made regarding improvements over the next three years, his plans to incorporate these changes through each of his chains, and so on. Then on his blog, you might see a comment from someone, a detractor, who spouts off that he is not satisfied by the amenities or service staff at a particular hotel. Not only is this the only comment of its kind, but it sticks out like a sore thumb; moreover, most everyone who reads it views it as inappropriate and will most often ignore it. Contrary to many executives' worst fear, not many will offer these types of comments because most realize how ineffective they are, especially when they are breaking the social norm.

In a discussion forum, the CEO could take what someone says and with one thread create a whole new separate, but related, conversation. Wiki's, again, are another story, because a co-editor can change what the CEO says and give everyone who reads the article a free room.

The simplicity of "wikistyle" self-publishing encourages initial contributions from a personal perspective. In this respect, it is quite similar to a blogging tool. But, perhaps more important because wikis make it simple to modify and reorganize existing information, encouraging a concept that is often referred to as "wiki gardening." Wiki gardening involves incrementally editing a wiki space to preserve continuity, make additional connections and links, and generally to clean it up.

Governance

In the corporate environment, the third property–governance–has vast implications, but for participants it simply involves an understanding of how the network maintains order. For our purposes, both governance managed both by the host and by the members can be successful as long as the rules are clear on both sides. If the host is governing your activities and content production, you should ensure that the regulations make sense and that nothing suspicious is going on. Activities to watch for include the unauthorized removal of posts and a lack of transparency in banning users. It's important that people know and understand the rules, which gives a sense of cohesiveness and unity, as well as an understanding about why someone is thrown out when they break these rules.

In same vein, in self-governance sites, you want to be sure that there are proper governing tools and functionality, for instance a 'report abuse' link, or the ability to regulate who sees and publishes your content. There also should be a place on the site where users have the ability to publish self-regulating laws or a network credo–a Code of Conduct. Finally, check the Terms of Use agreement to see what they do with your private information and the content you create. Who owns it? What rights do you have? This might sound trivial now, but it's good to understand implications for participation. To check terms of service policies, go to tosback.org.

Trust

Trust is the glue that holds it all together. In order to cash in on social capital, and to be an effective networker, you need confidence in the other party. It may be helpful to think of trust as the willingness to take risks. When you are forming a network of business associates, the risk at hand is to engage in a relationship even when you can't predict the behavior of your future partner.

Will they steal your idea, take credit for your work, or not reciprocate equitably? All of these things will likely come to mind, and that's natural. This is where your diligence in research comes into play.

If networks are designed to be a pool for initiating more defined or narrowly scoped groups, trust must be explicitly supported. As in the offline world, there are ways to intuit whether a person can be trusted. And, while these methods are not foolproof, typically, by doing your own research, and asking third parties for their insights, you can establish the nature of another person's reputation to a point of knowing whether you want to create a weak tie with them or not. Keep in mind, just as with people, networks should be evaluated to determine the types of people they attract.

Helpful features to recognize are as follows:
- referable testimonials and history/archives of behavior and ratings
- application process to join or verification of personal profile information

Features to be weary of include:
- anonymous activity (posts and comments without having to login)
- non-transparent rating and scoring systems

Social Networking

Social networking characteristics, like a profile, help people establish an online presence in order to build social networks–remember the various ways MySpace profile pages were personalized? A profile has one ultimate purpose: the explicit representation of self. With the pervasiveness of SBS, various networks now have flexibility and can approach social relationships differently than they ever could before, building a tighter correlation between a person's intended purpose for being in the network and the relationships they seek to establish; still a profile is a fundamental requirement.

All social networks, regardless of the surrounding noise like feeds and widgets, are essentially about people and their connections. This is integral because smaller groups are only as effective as the reach, but large networks of weak ties are only as effective as your ability to manage them. This can be a challenge when your network is too large– even with all the tools available. Bands and movie stars may benefit from thousands of random friends and connections. The rest of us generally don't.

Old School

Networks without social networking features still exist. While SBS is on the horizon, not everything has been converted. It is more challenging to create relationships within standalone social media, portals, and some blogs than it is with SBS. This is because they require additional time commitments and investments to find out who the other participants are.

Where SBS enables implicit relationships to help expedite the building of a network, these older networks, at best, only support explicit relationships. In these older networks, you assign and then select/build/approve potential ties–a very time-consuming process. Connections, or weak ties, are not impossible. Still, in some situations, these networks require supplemental tools, such as widgets and IM (Instant Messenger), or some sort of manual intervention to build a broader set of relationships. SBS continues to find ways to connect through existing contacts, common purpose, similar backgrounds, etc.

Ready to Participate

As you have read, SBS is a synergistic apparatus that blends the benefits of online communities–communication, collaboration, like-minded people, and a common purpose–with the benefits of social networking sites–relationship modeling, reputation, capability for trust, and initiating new relationships. This new confluence of tools is a vehicle for solid value and minimal risk.

Yet again though–none of this matters if you do not participate. Remember, participation and the Me Paradox are not about you. But they start with you. You have to take the initiative to actively participate, to put yourself in touch with the right networks, the right opportunities. You need to put yourself in a position to succeed.

In the following chapters, we will explore the ways to make SBS work for you by building coalitions of cooperation. But first, we must learn to find, select, and evaluate the most appropriate networks for your purposes.

~chapter six~
Online Networks

Relax. Put your feet up. No need for a pencil and paper in this section, but I do get a bit technical as we dive into the theory and the technology behind the scenes of social business. Just trust me when I say there are reasons for doing it. And, if it doesn't all become crystal clear to you here, it will later as we put these tools into practice.

We submerged ourselves in online presence and now your profile elements are contained in your Profile Framework spreadsheet. With this background and these tools, we will now explore the landscape and define the terrain where you will be operating.

The goal of this phase will be to adapt and conform to the network and interaction strategies that fit most appropriately to your personal tastes and objectives. Phase two of the online reputation lifecycle revolves around network strategy development.

Read carefully and follow the guidelines in the order described. For instance, you can't start gaining social capital or even exert the labor until you find a network that aligns with and contributes to your overall online reputation. Sure, you can visit Amazon or Yelp and review your favorite book or restaurant, but when it comes to reputation building, implicit currency like social capital is not something you can exchange just anywhere. The value depends on where you earn it and where you decide to spend it.

Think about it this way, in North Korea or deep in the South American Amazon, your American dollar is worth zero. And in England and Switzerland, your dollar is worth less than it's worth in the United States. You want to develop social capital, especially as you begin, that can be built and spent in the appropriate network or country. And just like the bills in your wallet, some will accept it as is while others will require you to exchange it, which many times is weighted against the exchange rate of the local currency. Social capital, along with the other parts of the social business construct, are why we take the time to understand and research the most appropriate networks before we select the one(s) best suited for us.

Network Classification

The best settings for professional growth are those that incorporate learning, extension of networks, and career opportunities. The methodology to achieve these goals includes classification, discovery, and evaluation.

The classification system is basic and easy to remember. It starts at the macro level, and the first attribute is access.

Access

When you land on a network page, the first thing you'll notice is whether or not you have access. If you have immediate access, you are in an un-gated network. Most social networking sites are un-gated, meaning there are no restrictions as to who can join or when. Because they rely on the number of users and the volume of traffic, limits would not make sense. They are also typically registration-based sites, where a person simply fills out a form to join the network. Registration is not subject to approval or moderation by another user, and once an account is activated, a user can add friends or content. While the registration process is usually succinct, some forms contain optional questions ranging from previous employers to favorite hobbies. These questions are all designed to enable online social networking.

Unfortunately, it is not always clear which information is required and which is optional. Beyond the username and password, a potential user needs to determine how much information is required to achieve assimilation with the existing networks so that social networking and relationship building activities may take place. Since the answers aren't always clear, rely on intuition and use your best judgment.

In some gated social networking sites, an existing connection to a user is required before membership can be obtained. Picture moving to a small, but prosperous, town and wanting to meet the movers and shakers to get your business off the ground. You attend the local chamber of commerce meetings, you join the Rotary Club, but you are having a hard time making headway because there are a lot of cliques. These people know each other well, and there's just not a huge welcome mat for newcomers.

Gated Networks

Gated sites can be similar. For instance, to become a member of Late Night Shots, a non-member would need to have to a friend or colleague who is already a member send them an invitation to join the site. As in most initiation rituals, this requires someone to put their reputation on the line and vouch for you. This accountability concept existed long before the Internet, but online it is designed to keep the number of inactive accounts or profile abandonments low. It also serves to increase the pace and intensity of ties members make.

The most coveted Social Business Sites are the gated ones. Admission makes members respect the network and treat others positively. You don't need mountains of research to tell you that the exclusivity enables quicker and tighter bonds, and gives each member a part in a network-wide commonality.

Establishing a link with another user on this type of network often requires the user to make a public declaration of accountability. For example, on Spoke, a user sends an e-mail invitation message to a non-user, which, if accepted, creates a connection. There are also sites on the other side of the spectrum. Word of Mouth is a network that does not require both users to register with the site to establish a link. The link is established by simply entering the e-mail address of the person you wish to link with, even if they are not members yet.

Gated networks are the most desirable because the benefits are many and the disadvantages are few. But not everyone has access, and like the old adage, it often becomes a situation of 'who you know, not what you know'.

Nonetheless, most gated networks are still likely very interested in reaching critical mass per their business model. They are not going to let everyone in, but they are building viral pathways through invitations and events, email campaigns, and membership drives as a method to reach out to a targeted crowd.

Joining a site like aSmallWorld[1] is similar to paying thousands of dollars to a country club or an athletic club and reaping the benefits of this exclusive place in society, with one major contingency: aSmallWorld doesn't necessarily care how much money you have in the bank. It's invitation only and you must know someone to get in.

This exclusivity adds value. It takes a lot of time and effort or money to find a patron who has the ability to invite you. This vetting process acts as a social lubricant for the network.

These movers and shakers are aware that their networks will only survive if they can capitalize on the network effect–reaching a large number of the right people. Access into some of these networks like American Chemical Society, American Medical Association, Intel

Channel, CIO Community, Cisco Marketing Group, etc., requires an invitation or some sort of pre-qualification to access.

So what does that mean for you? The first step is to determine the barrier to entry. As you go through the methods for finding a network, keep this in mind: the harder or more exclusive the network, the richer the benefits. This applies as long as there are a large number and diverse group of members. And, besides, how hard can it be? It's a social network, after all...

Upsides and Downsides

Even all this exclusivity has its downside, which you should consider before setting this type of goal. In these gated networks, most of the content is behind a firewall or secured wall that is not accessible by external users, bots, or search agents, all of which add to your online reputation. There is also a heightened sensitivity and obligation to the social norms, which can act as an impediment to change and prevent a broader diversity of knowledge within the network. This phenomenon is referred to as 'groupthink' and it essentially says, "hanging out with a bunch of elitists makes you an elitist."

It's nice to conform or have a sense of common purpose, thought, and vocabulary to help us assimilate with the group. However, after a while, this groupthink mentality can get in the way of thinking independently and open-mindedness, which might lead you to ostracize yourself from other networks you belong to. It's that clique mentality, and now you have become a member of the clique. Then again, if you belong to a gated network like aSmallWorld, you may not need to build your online reputation to the extent that the rest of us do.

Assessing a Network's Business Model

How the host chooses to make money and sustain the network forces certain decisions on the types of activities the network will promote and how it will behave. A business model has an input, an output, and environmental impacts. It also has a strong influence on the culture. For precautionary reasons, the intentions of the host must be known. For instance, ad-based businesses are counting on the traditional web metrics such as page views and unique visits, meaning that their focus will be driven by allowing viral types of communications. This creates a culture where connections and relationships dominate, where the push to have more contacts and more friends underpins every activity. Existing bonds–the ones created prior to joining–are unaffected and newly created bonds are weak in proportion to the sheer number of ties allowed. Contrarily, in a research and development network, where the business model is to develop and innovate, collaboration becomes a challenge as the number of people participating continues to grow. Ideation networks such as this are about quality, not quantity. And, their focus involves creating a culture of exclusivity and stronger bonded ties.

A hodgepodge of different types of gated and un-gated networks exist within various business models. You have to choose the best for you, based on your career goals, all while keeping the Me Paradox in mind.

Online Revenue Model

Understanding the business model will help you to evaluate whether or not a network is the right match for you. In addition, it helps you identify if a network is likely to survive or not. You do not want to choose a network that has little chance of survival and have all your hard work and content go down the drain with it.

Advertising is the new revenue model online. It has changed many online activities for the better and a few for the worse. Beyond helping an increasing amount of content and tools to be free, it affords a possibility for many smaller and more independent websites to survive, and in some cases thrive. Google AdSense is one obvious example of monetizing, say, a blog. Still, the chances of network survival is low for ad-based sites since the amount of traffic necessary to support a business with purely ad revenue is huge, and subsequent resources to sustain such a huge network are quite costly. The exception is found when the network is company funded or the content itself is valuable, like CNN's iReport, for instance. Reliance on ad-based revenue makes web traffic the network's highest priority, regardless of its stated purpose.

Network Discovery

The word is spreading about the benefits of being a network member, and people are becoming passionate about the networks they join. According to a 2008 report conducted by the Center for the Digital Future at the USC Annenberg School for Communication:

- Membership in online communities has more than doubled in only three years.
- 54% of online community members log into their community at least once a day.
- 55% of users say they feel as strongly about their online communities as they do about their real-world communities.

Community, as defined, is not bound to just SBS. It is a blog, an industry news publication portal, and it is a discussion forum. It is any combination of venues where you have the option of participating on the social web.

Having content in multiple networks is a strategy that involves generating content that can be directly and indirectly referenced/linked /tied to you and your presence. It is a way of getting relevant reputation-building information to be included in the hits when your name or area of expertise is searched. Just like your profile, your content needs a home as well.

PERSONAL STICKINESS ASSESSMENT

You might be asking yourself what I mean by personal stickiness. Well, I am not talking about a pancake syrup disaster, but rather a reputation that is unforgettable. It is about understanding what you are passionate about, what you are best at, or the place where you know the most people.

This is going to require a new way of thinking about:
- creative and diverse ways to embed yourself in relation to others
- opportunities for building weak and intermediate-strength ties, as follows:
    - ties that will play significant roles in providing us with professional opportunities
    - ties that will help us define this part of our professional identities
    - ties with potential sources for peer support and mentorship

There are many people who don't believe in search. Yes, we all use search, but even Google can fail us. This happens because, at times, we are not 100% sure what we are looking for. In fact, the way others behave, participate and interact online is more likely to drive search results than the phrase or words you use to search. Sites like Del.icio.us and Digg are founded on this principal.

Personal stickiness is a term used in response to the noise that comes with SPAM, SPLOGS, and web attacks. Personal stickiness is all about taking advantage of what you like and connecting with people who like the same things. And, if you are unique and your interests are unusual, that might just translate into a competitive advantage.

Here's an example: Say you are an editor. You have a few folks that you would like to call "connections" in the business world. You don't really know them yet, but you've established quite a following on the online book club you became actively involved in a couple years ago. While it is not a professional network by most standards, you have already established connections, testimonials, as well as group opportunities, so that might be the best place to start. When your name is out there it adds credibility and helps build your brand.

Search engines play an integral role as they are the engine most of us use to do our people searching, investigating, and subsequently, brand development. Search engines are the adhesive that bonds your online presence and your online activity via networks.

A composite of your search engine results may show only glowing responses to the type of books you like, the type of intense bonds you have made, and you may even find other supplemental content housed in another network. Now this is just one type of scenario, but the point is, you have clout and you could use that clout to develop weak ties–these weak ties could be transferred to (and from) other networks, if appropriate.

Personal stickiness is about looking all around you and recognizing the resources or interests you have, as well as your own unique aspects as it pertains to your job, education, skills, etc. It is also about taking a step back, looking at all the information around you, and recognizing what makes you happy.

Internal Social Media

Many large and small companies have adopted some sort of social media tool for internal or external use. In late 2008, SelectMinds conducted a survey[2] and from the responses, they were able to garner a list of reasons why companies have chosen to adopt a social media tool:

- Enhanced internal branding with employees
- Better brand ambassadorship within the employee base (how the organization is represented by its employees to their friends, families and acquaintances)
- Enhanced external branding with constituents involved in the Corporate Social Network
- Enhanced corporate culture
- Enhanced productivity
- Increased employee retention
- Increased motivation
- Increased new business opportunities
- Increased goodwill

There is a good chance these tools are already being employed within your organization. A great place to start is your current environment. By knowing that these exist and integrating this knowledge into your overall online reputation strategy is step one and it is the right approach.

In Gartner's Predicts 2007,[3] Gartner reports, "Enterprise social software will be the biggest new workplace technology success story of this decade."

There may be reasons why you do not want to get involved. Perhaps you are practicing in an environment that has potentially huge ramifications (good and bad). Perhaps you have a different persona at work as opposed to your social network online. Maybe you perceive it as a young person's tool? But whatever your reason, consider this: Not many of us have a choice if we hope to survive in the digital culture.

That's pretty blunt. But I am here to tell you the truth, and help you find ways to incorporate these realities into your own life.

Blogs

It seems that nearly everyone has a blog these days, and they are not all treated equally. By now you know what a blog is. Well, let's hope that you do. If not, it will be discussed in depth in the next chapter. According to famed publisher and technology thought leader, Tim O'Reilly,[4] 93 percent of the world knows what a blog is. A blog is an important vehicle for finding and even developing your network.

For our purposes here, we will use blogs as the source of information–a way station of sorts that gives us reprieve from the noise of search engine searches. A few years ago only thought leaders, those who were considered to be experts within a certain field, used them professionally.

So what does this mean to you? Well, first you have to find a blog that is representative of your industry, expertise, or organization. This is easier said than done. There is a proliferation of useless content and SPLOGS, which have grown exponentially in recent years. In addition, publishers are often regurgitating content that is already out there–not many are originators. Knowing an originating source, or getting as close as we can get to them, the better.

To identify the blogs in your space, start a search at a blog aggregator like Technorati, Blogpulse, or Daypop. You should be able to narrow down what you are looking for based on a category search. If you are very familiar with the topic and the thought leaders in your area, go straight to Google and do a search there. You also can track down your media or press lists and compare the names of the persons writing press releases. Google them to see if they are blogging as well.

One quick way to find whether a blogger is worth reading is to check the last post date and make sure it is relatively recent–I say relatively recent because some industries move slower than others, and there is simply not enough going on to report every day or even each week. In addition to this, also check what the web thinks of them by plugging the URL into Alexa and Urlfan–this should start to give you a good picture of who this blogger is relative to your industry.

Now, check their blogrolls. This is a list of favorite blogs read or referenced daily; these are found off to the side and are sometimes called by other names, like 'my favorite bloggers' or 'who I read'. Read their blogrolls, see who is reading who and very soon you start to see the nuts and bolts of the operation. Start collecting the names of people on the blogroll and then search them. Read some blog posts. It takes a lot of grunt work to find the nuggets (links and names of networks), but the effort is worth it. Slowly (in open and some gated communities), the names will begin to emerge and will lead you to these hidden jewels. You won't necessarily recognize the network's URL right away, but if the person you are searching has their name in that URL you have a better chance that it is in an SBS as well. If people's names are likely duplicates, use some distinguishing keywords or titles–similar to what you learned earlier–in the search phrase, like 'Peter Ford Cisco Engineer'.

In many ways, blogs will be one of your most important resources. Believe it or not, you too could soon be blogging, so take the time to familiarize yourself with the various blogging features and styles.

SBS Vendors

If you don't have a Facebook account then you are late to the party. Grandma might have just mastered email two years ago, but even she has hopped on the Facebook train and has discovered its usefulness in connecting with friends and relatives. It is becoming more apparent that social networking and user-generated content applications have rapidly changed the consumer world and its perception of online technologies.

These technologies are also affecting the enterprise work environment. Evidence suggests that businesses have shown a great deal of interest in these applications as a way to improve interactions and to gain ad-hoc information not easily captured by more structured applications built around well-defined business processes. Companies realize that social business software, or SBS, can support broader business initiatives by building communities of employees, partners, and customers. While the goals of each community may vary, the underlying social business mechanisms provide the power to better connect people to information and to one another. Companies have realized the potential of these technologies and are flocking to SBS platform vendors.

Available in the **End Notes** of this book[5] there is a sample list from Jive Software. The list is not comprehensive, in fact it's a couple years old, but it allows you to get a snapshot of the horizon in terms of the number of companies and the types of companies (large companies for that matter) that have already deployed SBS in one capacity or another.

When you multiply that number with the list of vendors out there–SalesForce, IBM, Microsoft, Oracle–you will come to realize that these vendors are selling an increasing number of platforms to customers who are producing more networks. Unlike blogs, which are standalone, these will be directly tied to the network. The result then is that searching vendors should lead you to companies that should lead you to the networks founded on their platform or interpretation of SBS.

In order to perform a vendor search, start at the vendor's corporate webpage and go to their clients/customers link/tab. Every vendor will have this. It is known in the industry as a 'must have' on your website. Within the customer tab, you will find companies highlighted, sometimes with links to the networks the vendor has created for them. In some cases, this will be a direct hit. In other cases, this will only have a client's name. Try to find a client that is a powerhouse in your industry. For instance, in lower education, a company like K12 might be important. From that you should know that K12 has deployed a network and now you have a lead to follow: 1) you can try various K12 Google searches, or 2) you can call K12 directly and ask about their network and how you can get involved. If this is a gated network and for those in this industry, it would be a great find since they provide distance education to the world through SBS and their network.

Another method is to join their support or their customer networks. At a minimum, you will gain access to pertinent information because most vendors encourage their customers to openly post questions, concerns, best practices, etc. In the industry, this is called 'eating your own dog food'. In addition, these networks provide access to webcasts and other activities that introduce the product, who is using it, and simply being a part of that network provides you with unique access that others who have not taken the time to study the world of social business will not be privy to. There are times that this information is held confidential, but if you navigate around, you will see how their particular network operates on the various SBS platforms.

Publicly Available

The consumer space of the social web is widely publicized. In a 2009 CNN article written by Stephanie Chen, Gina Bianchini, CEO of

Ning, says "[in Ning] there are 200,000 social networks active right now, and they are across tens of thousands of unique passions."

Even businesses are, at increasing numbers, using Facebook. This is evident by the sheer numbers of groups being set up in Facebook, sometimes as fan pages. Many organizations find Facebook a perfect place to practice before they go onto a more mature platform dedicated to their business purposes. If you go to Facebook and do a search for an interest group you will probably find dozens, maybe even hundreds. If you find a particular group of interest, you could follow this interest group because there is a high likelihood they will transition to an SBS network someday.

Meetup.com is another easy way to practice. Meetup is a website that allows users to search for others who share an interest and who are locally available to meet face-to-face. There is zero commitment and the barrier to entry is pretty low, so the abandonment of profiles is very high. This makes it a perfect place to practice, within reason of course.

Major players like Google, Microsoft, and Yahoo! also have groups. For instance, Yahoo! Groups is a directory where different group list themselves and become searchable for anyone interested in finding a group like theirs. These aren't hard-hitting methods, but they're valid and provide a good starting point.

What's available to the public is the broadest category of all. For anyone using this method, make sure you keep good records of the networks you do find and when you are ready, ensure you do an 'apples with apples' comparison using the evaluation methods defined later.

BEST PRACTICE REVIEW

Let's try an exercise in imagination, where the scene put forth is purely hypothetical in nature. Imagine that we are graphic designers trying to find the ideal network in order to build our reputations. So we start with Ning where we search the phrase "graphic designer."

This search produced more than 4,500 groups. Generally, we tend to look at the first few pages of groups and since we don't know how the search sorts the ordering, we start browsing by looking at group names, pictures and descriptions, and go with what appeals to us. We begin to see trends. We start to recognize the use of other more definitive words, such as "artwork," "publishing," etc.

We redo the search with each of these terms added to 'graphic designer', and we produce varying result sets, but these results are less than our original 4,500 groups. We evaluate some of the groups using what we have learned so far and add those we feel have potential, and then we go to Google.

On Google, we search the phrase "social networking graphic designer." This leads us to an organization blog called graphicdefine.org. We scan the blog and within there, an article emerges and leads us again to a design community called designerid.com. This seems much more like a professional network as opposed to a recreational one. As we profile peruse, we can tell by a few of the bios we read of the members and top participants that these are some of the folks we want to mingle with. Moreover, the topics they are discussing are interesting, useful, advanced, etc., and the site has overall appeal.

Now, let's compare this search with another profession you may also be unfamiliar with (and, if by chance you are familiar, just play along).

Search the phrase "social networking mechanical engineering" to find results specific to the field. This search returned a number of articles and a directory of networks. A particularly interesting one was mechdir.com–an SBS directory which has a variety of other forums, SNS, and communities. Many SBS are small, open, and with ad-based business models. If you see potential, add these to your list. Back to Google, we do another search, this time using the phrase "online community mechanical engineering" and this returns the mecca of engineering communities. The first to show up is SolidWorks.[6] They are a respected name in the industry, get plenty of traffic, have great search engine optimization, and back links. If you were to make this part of your network and engage, it would do wonders for your online reputation.

Network Selection Guidelines

Once you start seeing these lists of potential networks, you begin to realize the importance of classifying and evaluating the networks you join and, most importantly, the ones you participate in. There are hundreds of networks and categories, from professions to religions to hobbies. It is critical to find a professional network that fits your personality and your unique needs.

Realize, this might come at a cost, whether it's time or money.

We will make these evaluations at different phases and apply the factors in stages. As you begin to gain familiarity with making similar assessments on a multitude of levels, the theory will become more tangible and applicable for you.

The value of a network increases exponentially as it expands, access is broadened and new members are added. But you need to evaluate and determine the point when your inclusion and participation becomes effective? You can join a network and gain contacts to a thousand 9th graders, but unless you are a pop star, the chances of those contacts being of value to you are slim.

Professional Impact

We evaluate networks by their worthiness and merit, finding that balance between the right network for your personality and goals, with the longevity and prosperous nature of the network itself. The market has shown that both are required to make it worthwhile. It is not about joining Facebook and throwing up a profile on LinkedIN, and then calling it quits. Finding and evaluating SBS is a pretty big undertaking, and much of this wealth is just not available as a lurker. You need a proper balance of risk and effort as you work to make this discovery.

The sanctity of shared interest is common among alumni networks, technical user forums, and gated networks. If you have to pay, be a member, or be invited, you are going to have an easier time integrating. That's one side of the spectrum. On the other side is Facebook, a context-driven network with no barriers to entry where all relationships are pre-existing or loosely created and have varying levels of value.

You can adopt a few different networks, but more than three is not advised. If a network has all the right characteristics and the benefits are not apparent, investigate to determine the reasons why. Sometimes it just takes awhile. Sometimes you have benefitted but it is not apparent yet. This could be a weak tie, a potential business partner, or someone determining your leadership position in your area of expertise. It could also be someone who would gain by positively affecting or influencing your career. This is not about the 'one in a million chance', this is social business and the Me Paradox.

As part of the engagement phase, **Chapter 9** will discuss how to approach your new network but for now just realize that there are no shortcuts, just hard work and the first mover advantage.

Just as in the real chaotic world, you need to be open-minded and flexible. For example, at first glance, there may not be the conversations you are interested in or the network itself may not have the professional impact you are looking for, but with the right people or even the right context, there may still be plenty of opportunities. Have you ever heard of weak ties? Weak ties are foreign by nature, and most often the opportunities they hold are not obvious. By operating within the Me Paradox, activities like network development are implemented with purpose, which drives stickiness and activates increasing network effects.

Network Evaluation

Now it is time to start evaluating the different features of the various networks on your list. There are three general properties to consider:

- Organizational Culture
- Mechanisms of Function
- Network Viability

Organizational Culture

We, as humans, need to know who's who. It helps us as we identify ways to integrate and co-exist. We naturally build boundaries to identify who belongs and who doesn't. The foundation to these walls being put up is the trust among the members–who is it that we are engaging and is it safe to do so?

This is simply not an exercise of looking up someone's profile. Understand that it is hard to digitally model trust and thus, regardless of what is built around the user profiles, there are no guarantees. Therefore you have to evaluate the culture as a whole and, as many researchers have noted, social pressures are equally as powerful as, and sometimes even more powerful than any other form.

In addition, you are not really looking at functionality of blogs, wikis, and forums, but instead you look at ways the user can add richness to the network as a whole. Activity builds context about the environment and its purpose.

The ability to link between users and make connections creates a networked ecosystem of nodes, a connected group of individuals. Viewing and searching the history of activity is a great way to evaluate the culture of a network. The connections you will find are those that have occurred through common understanding and valuation of the implicit currency used in the network.

Awareness

By "awareness," I mean gaining insight into the many different types of networks that exist. For many kinds of networks and particularly those involving economy of regard activities, such as Internet commerce, software usage, information, or special-interest knowledge, the more extensive a network becomes, the more valuable it is likely to be. However, for some activities, like research and development (R&D) collaboration, networks that grow too large may experience diseconomies. These may occur because of higher interaction and coordination costs as communications increase, or due to leaks of new innovations to competitors as the network grows larger.

Be aware of your network type offline and then compare it to the online network. How do they compare? Is it the same or more focused offline? This definitely speaks to the maturity of the online network. If the online network, with all its advantages, cannot compete from a membership reach level, this network may not be ready for your involvement. Evaluate whether a network is mature, wide, and diverse before diving in.

Competence

People in communities naturally organize themselves into smaller subgroups. Forming groups is a necessary and organic process–it's what humans do. And this is where the competence factor becomes more apparent. The entire network might be composed of competent members, but if the group you form is the 1 percent of incompetent people, then you have a problem. Moreover, if I am the most competent, do I really want to join this network? You need to recognize the competence level of the network from a larger and then smaller subset. Both do not need to have the same results. For instance, in an incompetent network, a smaller more competent group may be enough to get you to your goals. Focus on identifying the competence levels and, as you build your engagement plan, this factor will play a role in your decisions.

Benevolence

Dilution of hierarchies is the current trend with any professional workplace. For our purposes, dilution means that the power or authority at some (or all) levels of a hierarchy may be diminished as participants find themselves able to interact or transact more freely with one another. People who sit at the top have less of a social responsibility relative to their reach. They view your access to them as more charity than a true collaboration where every participant brings value and has a value proposition. At an essence, the less of a hierarchy the better the benevolence factor. Be weary of titles and statuses not purposed for expert designation and network contributions.

Networks tend to dilute hierarchies, as access is opened up and established levels of control disappear. Why is this important? Look at the world today and how you operate within it. The loss of hierarchy may increase the scale of a network and its returns because participation and the freedom it provides attract more members. People are more apt to help each other when the motivations are transparent. At the same time, building trust is more of a prevailing exercise. Access to collaboration and personal information is freely available to all in the network.

Motivation

The network purpose may differ from the preferred activity, but if the community is about innovation and ideation, yet it is being used as a dating site, this is a pretty clear sign that the culture is more social, and it is apt to ignore the over-arching directive and calls to action.

It's important to identify the motivation of the network. It is nearly impossible to know another person's motivation, but the research process should prepare you to evaluate intelligently. From a broad perspective, you can see signs of mutual motivation very clearly by looking at number of connections people have. It makes one start to wonder what type of currency is being traded. Many of us love a good murder mystery because with enough information, you can always tell who did it. In the same way that you would read and evaluate a murder mystery, you will attempt to find out what type of currency is being exchanged and how that will lead to the motivation. This will also help as it pertains to determining what your own motives are. What do you want from a network and its members?

Access

You need to recognize why you open yourself up to others and, in turn, you need a good understanding of why someone would choose to reveal themselves to you. This often becomes another question about the type of currency that is being exchanged. Social capital can be exchanged for contacts, prestige, and so on. Access is very similar to motivation, but the distinction lies in the focus of personal relations. Underneath the hood, good standing membership coupled with strong limits to network growth or capacity enables these connections to occur. There are, however, some questions to consider as you evaluate the network's access:

- Who and how do you ask for something?
- Are you willing to give what the network is asking for—is there enough return (knowledge, contacts, friendship, etc.)?
- Does the culture reward connections?
- How do the members view goodwill?
- Will it create new business opportunities?
- Will it increase productivity?

These factors do not differ from the general altruism members tend to extend to other members. One story I'd like to share is about one of the most respected professions in the world—doctors. In the process of assisting the American Medical Association and its 500,000 members, some interesting facts emerged about the behaviors and attitudes these medical professionals have towards their profession and their peers.

The most striking is regarding competition. Doctors, rather than compete against other doctors, welcome them. The act of passing the trials of schooling and board certification was a right of passage, which created camaraderie, not competition. Another interesting fact that emerged is that doctors often feel a sense of isolation and have trouble finding like-minded peers to socialize with. A large majority had numerous friends, but many conveyed that there were none they could truly relate to. Doctors sought out various ways to find like-minded peers, which provided a compelling argument for the AMA to establish a social business site.

A 2007 BioInformatics PJA survey[7] confirmed what the AMA already knew. Most doctors in a network were generally accessible to each other, even when they were unlike their peers in terms of age or specialty. In fact, doctors are among the busiest of professionals yet they found time for other doctors. The culture within the profession itself transcended the medium; anything could have been put in place besides SBS as long as it shortened the distance of access to someone they could relate to. This happily happened with SBS; it was much easier and fulfilling to connect with someone with the same pains and struggles as themselves.

Diversity

The word "collaboration" broadly blankets this concept, and encapsulates any talents a member or the network as a whole provides. The preferences and opinions of those participating and not participating are generally expressed as network identity. The transparency of each member's activities contributes to the whole. The perception of skills within a network is bound to the constraints of opportunities that exist. It makes sense that 'I' fill a role (say, secretary or organizer) that no one wants to do. If you do take on these roles that obviously downplay your true capabilities, in the overall interest of the group, will you be recognized for it?

Everyone has a niche that expresses itself either as part of a whole, or as an individual who doesn't understand the gains of synergy for a greater good.

Very simply, you want to make sure the network embraces and contains diversity. Then factor in the culture by asking whether or not the members are willing to take on roles for the greater good of the network as a whole. This will require an understanding of purpose.

Think in terms of team and this will help you to gauge the potentials and the value in store for you.

Mechanisms of Function

The technology spectrum is wide. There are listservs on one end and advanced social business software on the other. Knowing these tools and how they are used to enable the network is another important key to network evaluation.

First, consider the social business: what are people trading? Is it knowledge, support, goods, services, or ideas? This revelation should lead you to the features that enable the activity. For instance, it might be ratings associated with something traded, or the barriers to entry, or consensus needed for an idea's acceptance.

Next, look at the shared spaces in the environment. Every network needs a shared space. Is there a place for conversations? Amazon's comments and ratings are valuable but it is not a shared space. Instead, for those who are unaware, it is very deceptive. People post and those postings are grouped together. Then people are asked to rate the product regardless if they love it, hate it, or are just venting because of an impending divorce. Beyond the mechanism to reach out and communicate with each other, and understand who is actually making the comment via profile, we lack the appropriateness of a common goal. Why did you buy the product? How does that relate to your goals?

The best way to understand this shared space concept is by asking yourself not only what is *gained* (information on a product, for instance), but how that *translates* into social capital. For example, if I post a comment here, who will read it and then is there a mechanism to ask them a question in return, for instance, how much that comment helped them?

Finally, think about the governance of the network and the features that regulate it. We evaluated the culture and made sure that the shared and stated values are appropriate but how do the features help regulate this agreed upon behavior? For a network to work, communication and interaction must exist.

- How are members interacting and communicating?
- Is it all online?
- Are some members meeting offline?

The quickest way to discover and understand governance is to observe the communication and interactions of its members. If they use wikis, observe how they are correcting each other, and how they govern or moderate the group's content? Private messages, IM, offline interactions, and unregulated personal testimonials are highly prone to miscommunication and situations of he said/she said. Make sure the governance is network managed through auditable history. Very simply, what was said is viewable by all and therefore the freedom as well as the responsibility falls on the members.

Network Viability

Maybe you've thoughtfully considered every evaluation tactic but, if the network is not successful, your efforts, resources, and time spent could be lost.

In 2008, Gartner Research[8] evaluated criteria that make consumer networks like Facebook and Flickr successful. They demonstrated what enterprises should use as a macro guide to measuring their own SBS success.

The first criterion is volume, which very easily is seen as network growth. Volume is important because the higher the number of participants, the more content that is refreshed which translates into more interest and subsequently, more value. Additionally, a higher number of members means there is more diversity and the opportunities become more dynamic. First though ensure the network is growing or stable, has the resources within it to reach a higher growth rate, while maintaining a consistent sustainability.

Participation is the second criterion. Participation numbers can range from 10 percent to 20 percent of the total population–higher levels are generally associated with niche-type networks.

If most of the network is only about information retrieval, the content eventually gets stale and membership drops off. In addition, it is hard to meet and connect with people if most of them are only seeking information. The maxim 'you get out what you put in' resonates here. Members that put up a bare-bones profile and don't maintain their pages rarely participate or attract many people to join. Steer clear of this–you will find that their reach and influence tend to be small. Participants who actively get involved by contributing content and commenting on other people's postings get more responses in return, thereby improving overall content quality, relevance, influence, and satisfaction.

At the risk of being redundant, I will touch one more time on reputation as part of the next criterion. In general, users gain satisfaction from being known, well-regarded, and making connections. In order to allow a replacement for F2F meetings and encounters, a reputation mechanism must exist. Make sure you choose a network where you are able to grow your reputation, quantify it, and then validate it with the people and activities you perform.

The final criterion is weak ties. Who are those contacts that are not regulars in your life, but that you feel comfortable enough to ask a favor from and vice versa? Trust me, I realize this is sometimes more of an attitude change, but it is a new form of networking or relationship construct. If a network does not allow you to create, manage, and grow your weak ties then it will not be successful.

The network, as well as its members, must be working to grow weak tie connections otherwise the value is context-dependent, which can be random and unreliable. The effort you put in is for the people and not the content. Content is a positive by-product and could realistically be found anywhere. Information overload is a problem; knowledge is not. Weak ties turn information into knowledge or better.

Finding Neverland

Reputation plays an important role in society, and preserving the private details of one's life is essential to it. In a nutshell, reputation development is a complex process and should not be rushed, as it is vital to your success. Time is on your side. The first mover advantages are limited and the risks far outweigh the benefits, so be strategic. Take your time, even if you are job hunting. You still have time to prepare and plan according to your goals.

We are at the crux, and those who start now are at an advantage, not only for finding more opportunities but for preparing for the future. We need to find our niche and to be successful there, we need to match our resources with the niche's requirements.

You may not find the right network on your first try or even in the first several tries. Don't stress. Ultimately, when you are actively and smartly participating, if a network–your perfect network(s)–does exist, you will find it or rather, because you are working within the Me Paradox, it will find you. You are the beacon in the night. The lighthouse on the distant shore. People, when also practicing the Me Paradox, are always guided to that light.

~chapter seven~
Economy of Regard

What is the economy of regard, and how does that relate to the Me Paradox?

The Me Paradox can be seen as a phenomenon where what you want for yourself, you get for someone else. If you want a job, help find a job for someone else. If you want to be rich, help someone else get rich. Like all adages and quips we hear today, there are much deeper implications than the generalization exemplifies. Nevertheless, when you boil it down, it is as simple as *you get what you put in-to people*.

On the other hand, regard is a grant of attention and since attention is a limited resource, *The Economy of Regard*, coined by economist and Professor Avner Offer, is the market exchange of attention.[1] The basic premise is that self-regard is difficult to sustain without external confirmation, so it must be accumulated; this is the heart and soul of the Me Paradox. Without you regarding others and others regarding you, you operate in poverty with limited opportunities for trade, growth, and prosperity. Signs of this market exchange transformation are ever more present online.

In 2010, Facebook announced Open Graph API,[2] which allows you to put a 'like' button on any web page or site. You may ask, what is a 'like' button going to do when it is on every website? Think about it this way: for every like or mention, you have a citation, meaning if a cardio-thoracic surgeon or 10,000 individuals give a mention to a website that claims to have the best diet for your heart, you are going to listen. This is compelling evidence showing that something is what it says it is.

Someday soon, search engines like Google will have to further adapt to similar social signals, just like they did for links. Eventually, search engines will be driven purely by people, where the quantity and quality of regard that you have defines the type of information you get. To scale regard to the quantities required to sustain a prosperous career, you must harness and capitalize on your online reputation now.

Online reputation is a manifestation of the Me Paradox. Remember the *Online Reputation Lifecycle* in figure 7-1?

Figure 7-1

ONLINE REPUTATION LIFECYCLE

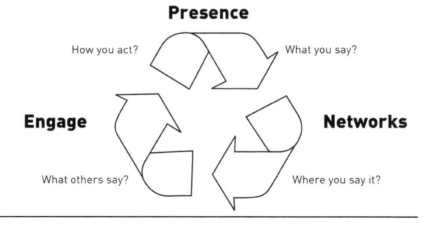

Since online reputation is tangible and the Me Paradox is not, what is evident in your online reputation signals how well you understand the economics of regard, or what you have come to know as social business.

A Mutual Trust

Building an online reputation is an investment of repeated use of carefully chosen but minimally taxing commitments. Creating that reputation is the first step to becoming integrated into the networks that open up these possibilities for you, and while it's a lot of reward for not a lot of investment, you have to understand how to make those investments; which is why only few people understand how to take advantage of the connections they build online.

For some people, making connections, or more specifically cooperation, comes naturally. They don't even realize what they're doing–they just do it, and it works. For the rest of us, cooperation is an effort, something that is thought out on the basis of different motives and emotions, and each situation has its own unique details to contend with. The nature of cooperation is complex, and an all-encompassing explanation has even defied researchers. But we do know that cooperative behaviors fall into two categories: *altruism* and *mutualism*.

As a concept, *altruism* is simple. Altruistic people do things selflessly, with no expectation of return from others. Let's be candid, though. The concept, in its purest form, is rare. It took over a decade of being the richest man in the world before Bill Gates became a philanthropist.

Cases of pure altruistic behavior are atypical and infrequent. In fact, too much altruism would have been maladaptive for human evolution. People who do give without expectation of return are often selective about how, or when, or to whom they give. They focus on the need, the cause, someone or something they can empathize or sympathize with. Even in these limited cases, altruism is only possible if individuals forego the narrow pursuit of self-interest for a greater good. For over a century, social scientists have argued that sympathy mitigates self-interest. But sympathy is fragile: the nature of the receiver can eliminate sympathy and make the prospect of altruism evaporate. You are not going to give a homeless person money if you feel like they are going to go spend it on alcohol or drugs, even though they plead that it is for food.

The fact is, people are naturally wary of relying on altruism because, as I mentioned before, there is so little genuine altruism. Often, something that looks like altruism has a hidden catch, an expectation of return that makes it something else entirely. A large portion of Dr. Robert Cialdini's work[3] explores the deceptive tactics employed by car salesmen, Hari Krishnas, and telemarketers, where a gift or a seemingly altruistic act is merely a ploy to create obligation. The underlying psychological principles obligate humans to cooperate in response to such acts of generosity, in which, more often than not, altruism is met with temporary cooperation.

Mutualism is more common, and a concept that is more likely to result in benefits for both parties. Cooperation is based on your similarities or shared interests, regardless of what you stand to gain. Both altruism and mutualism require trust, but mutualism actually requires more confidence because we need to be assured that our efforts will be met by the cooperation of the other party. In order for it to work, we need to believe that we will gain too. The transparency of signals and communication are the keys to mutualism because they're necessary to establish this level of trust to get two distinct parties to cooperate.

Once a relationship based on mutualism begins, both parties have "skin in the game," and it's easier to build and maintain that trust.

Of course, mutualism and altruism are not mutually exclusive. The motivating factors for most cooperative behaviors fall somewhere in between. But understanding these aspects is the key to making social business work. Both motivations for cooperation depend upon openness and transparency to strive for a win-win situation.

Coalition Building Through SBS

Coalitions are groups drawn together to cooperate. Sometimes they have very different motives, but are working toward a specific end–a variation of a win-win situation. One party may act altruistically, another mutualistically, and others with a blend of both; but together they form a **coalition**. Several studies have explored the nature of coalitions and coalition-building and the important implications for how we are using SBS.

Michael Watkins, in his book[4] designed to help leaders in new leadership roles, discusses coalition-building and creates a cycle (see figure 7-2) where you gain an ally, then this ally helps recruit another ally. Each ally brings in a resource base that adds to your own, whether that's financial resources, a support system, or simply the right kind of weak tie. This pooling of resources puts you one step closer to your goals. Now you're in a better position to recruit new allies, because you've demonstrated your success and increased your reputation.

Figure 7-2

COALITION BUILDING CYCLE

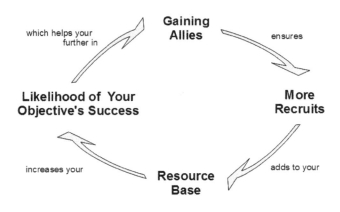

"The order in which you approach potential allies and convincibles will have a decisive impact on your coalition-building efforts," explains Jim Sebenius.[5] He calls this "sequencing strategy," which means if you find a reputable ally, it is now easier to recruit another reputable ally. Along the same lines, a non-reputable ally does not increase your chance of success nearly as much.

When starting a coalition, the first person you connect with makes the most impact. Be careful not to go down the path of least resistance and choose the most convenient ally. This does not mean later that you are prohibited from allying with anyone of your choosing, but initially you will want to be strategic and if possible, make your first connection with someone who is reputable. These insights provide us with an outline of aspects to consider when choosing an ally:

- Approach those with whom you already have some sort of supportive relationship established.
- Shoot for someone with compatible interests.

- Look for people who have the critical resources you need to achieve your goals.
- Choose those who have important connections–even a weak tie can be an important resource.

Building a strong coalition means getting people committed to cooperation, and mutualism is one surefire way to do that. Coalition-building is a cyclical process. There is a tight correlation to achieving your professional goals or excelling at social business and perpetuating the coalition-building cycle through positive feedback or reciprocation from contacts.

The Evolution of the Marketplace

This concept is not only for your workplace, but for your actions on the Internet as well. The authors of *Cluetrain Manifesto* have a compelling take on coalition building. Their perspective is indicated in what they describe as The Marketplace. In the authors' words, "the first markets were markets. Not bulls, bears, or invisible hands. Not battlefields, targets, or arenas. Not demographics, eyeballs, or seats. Most of all, not consumers." Here, they emphasize the idea of a marketplace not as an abstract construction that is tracked in econometric statistics, but as the literal place: the market square, where people go to buy and sell and do so much more. Along with the chickens and cheese, there was another, perhaps just as important, item being exchanged: Information.

Thousands of years ago, without the ability to flip on the evening news, click a mouse, or even open a newspaper, people craved information, as it was critical for survival. And the only place they could obtain that information was to get it from other people. Information wasn't some advertising pitch created for a nameless, faceless crowd. It wasn't filtered or spun or predigested into headlines.

It was a background thread woven into business, friendship, and daily interactions. Information didn't have its own highway. It moved as people moved. Anthropologists have traced information through folklore by following the long distance routes and information exchanges that took place in the spice trading industry, dating back to 1550 B.C.

Information about the latest innovation to make life easier or life-saving medical discoveries from distant lands was extremely valuable because there was no mechanism to mass produce it. The printing press wasn't an option then as it wasn't invented until a few thousand years later. Even in these times, it was clear that not only was information valuable, but information, as something traded, had different value depending on who was involved. It depended upon the context: A new story comes to town, but who generated it? Is it the reliable salt merchant, or a tinkerer you've never seen before? Would you take an unknown root as medicine for a stomach ache from someone you had no relationship with? You might be in extreme pain, but you realize the wrong kind of root or plant could kill you. Human nature hasn't changed much. What has changed is the means by which we communicate and share ideas, the means by which we consume information.

Information Consumption

It's easy to imagine information as something that is passively consumed, like watching the nightly news. But even today, information can't be severed from its context, from the relationships going on behind the scenes, whether those relationships are between you and a customer or you and the friends who discuss the same late-night show the next day. You choose what to watch based on who produces it, yes, but, perhaps inadvertently, you also choose it based on what others are watching. The "most popular" list on the sidebar of CNN's website wasn't created in a vacuum.

Of course, we all have the choice to be passive consumers, but that puts us at the mercy of others who are engaging with our information as well as those who supply it. Active consumers know that their behavior is practically a requirement for getting anything done. Think about when the term "market" became a verb. Most of us don't recall exactly when the word also came to mean an activity you do to attract a customer. But Cluetrain authors describe that moment as a revolution in industry. That's a realization of the role of relationships in social business–the effect cooperation and coalitions have on the exchange of information.

The Me Paradox is put into action by you, and it works through the reciprocation of others.

Circle of Contacts

The social web is a medium and a context that breaks down many traditional barriers often cited as reasons a contact has been lost such as changing jobs or where you live.

Significant changes in our lives tend to happen about every seven years, and for similar reasons, a contact is likely to have about the same lifespan. Studies[6] have shown that we lose about half of our contacts every seven years, and part of that loss, as well as the creation of new ones, is dependent upon our changing opportunities to interact, our available time, for instance, or our location, our job, and so on. Contacts don't happen because a random force pushes two people together; they're not the result of fate, or randomness, or a higher cause. Contacts happen because opportunities to meet influence the social composition of our personal networks. The ability to make contacts is context-driven, so putting yourself in the right context is the first step to generating those contacts that are most valuable to you.

Making Lasting Connections

Along those same lines, people choose friends for various reasons. A 2001 study by McPherson[7] and other researchers showed that in the United States, friendships in the last century were formed due to commonalities or key factors. These included, in decreasing order, race and ethnicity, age, religion, educational level, occupation, and gender.

On the Internet, social media can radically change our available opportunities to meet and connect with others. These days, we're not limited to our neighbors or bound by proximity. This has huge implications for why and how you participate online. Deciding to participate, and choosing the right networks, can influence how many opportunities will open up for you to make crucial connections.

Think of a homeowners association meeting with thousands of members that are all potential contacts or relationships. These online relationships, or "weak ties," work differently. The phrase itself may imply that these weak ties are not worth the effort, but that is not the case, especially when we're trying to get integrated into a group and build a network that has real value.

Distinguishing Between Tie Strengths

Mark Granovetter, from Stanford, and Caroline Haythornthwaite are two of the leading researchers on transforming social capital into professional goodwill using new media. They discuss three kinds of ties: strong ties, weak ties, and latent ties.

Latent ties are those that exist because of the technology and the infrastructure that enables social business; these are people in a network whom you haven't met yet, but easily could. You can initiate contact with them either because you have a common acquaintance or because you already have a connection mediated by technology–it's just not yet a direct connection. I won't discuss latent ties in detail because once you understand the implications of weak ties, the properties of latent ties will make more sense.

Both strong and weak ties are interpersonal. To differentiate between the two, Granovetter defines the strength of a tie as a combination of the following:

- amount of time invested,
- emotional intensity, the intimacy (mutual confiding),
- reciprocal services that characterize the tie.

Although these factors are "somewhat independent," they are highly correlated; if you spend a lot of time with someone, it's likely you will have greater intimacy and more emotional intensity in that relationship, and vice versa. Each factor has its own measures, but they tend to be related. Even one measure being different may not affect the overall strength of the tie. For instance, you may have a family member you do not confide in, but the emotional intensity and the amount of time spent make for a strong bond overall. Conversely, it is tough to be intimate with someone if you don't spend enough time with them. Or, if they are unwilling to have a mutual exchange with you, the emotional intensity is lessened. Family, friends, and co-workers on a project all represent strong ties as do a department head and the department staff. Professionally, strong ties are forged because small groups of people in similar jobs interact on a regular basis.

Laying a Foundation with Weak Ties

Think about who is on your speed dial or who has the most email exchanges with you. These are likely to be your strong ties. Those who have strong ties with each other tend to have similar experiences and attitudes because they travel in the same circles. Strong ties are also more likely to have a high level of intimacy and self-disclosure. We have relatively few strong ties because there just aren't enough hours in the day to maintain that kind of contact with more than a few people. Most importantly, strong ties tend to have a high exchange rate or an inclination to share what resources they have with each other. This is because their social circles, backgrounds, and status are often relatively similar. Strong ties are nice to have, but they are not as professionally valuable to you due to their similarity to you.

Weak ties are contacts, acquaintances, friends of friends, and so on: anyone that you have limited contact with but still maintain some sort of linkage to. A variety of disparate people have only occasional exposure to each other, or some kind of indirect relationship. You might think of these as "nodding acquaintances" because you say hello when you see each other, but you don't share the details of your day. Examples might include engineers and salespeople for the same organization, or executives and front-line customer service employees who commonly work in different geographies or product areas.

Weak ties generally are geographically dispersed, racially or ethnically different, vary in profession, have a different educational background, and have financial disparities. In a relationship with only weak ties, each of the above listed factors contributing to the forming of friendships is less likely to be identical, including age and gender. These differences contribute to making the ties superficial and harder to maintain. The interesting phenomenon that begins to surface in the Me Paradox is that weak ties with people who are significantly different from you are some of your greatest resources.

The Strength of Weak Ties

Alan Ross created a successful career for himself in academic publishing, but when his youngest daughter left for college, he started to wonder if it might be time to make a change. He had no idea how to make that happen, though. He started studying to be a physicist, but decided after obtaining his master's degree that the field had lost its initial appeal. The competitive, soul-crushing grind of working on "big science" projects run by somebody else through years of doctoral and post-doc programs just had lost its luster. He had taken a side job proofreading questions and answers in high-school physics textbooks, and he turned that into a full-time job, eventually writing his own successful textbook after realizing his own unexpected talent for writing about complex ideas for a teenage audience.

After several years and three editions of his own book, he began to find the routines of academic publishing almost as mind-numbing as the endless runs and re-runs of computer analyses that he performed during his brief time in a major laboratory. Alan had spent his free time lately by writing a novel, trying to play with the potential of introducing high-school and college students to intermediate physics concepts through what was, essentially, a murder mystery. His daughter told him it helped her get through her own physics classes, but he thought she might have been just her stroking her old man's ego. He toyed with the idea of submitting the manuscript for publication, but his confidence level was such that he thought it would be a waste of time.

Then things changed when he accidentally ran into Marissa, a neighbor in his apartment complex. She was dumping huge piles of pages into the recycling bin, threatening to overflow the canister before he had the chance to throw in his small pile of soda cans. Marissa apologized, and explained that she had brought home part of her publishing company's "slush pile," a stack of unsolicited manuscripts–the bane of busy editors. Alan knew from casual conversation that Marissa worked at the local branch of a big fiction publisher. The size of that slush pile was intimidating enough that he imagined submitting his draft novel would be useless.

As Alan gently stuffed his cans into empty spaces, trying not to cause a paper avalanche, Marissa made small talk. She told him how she was always halfway between laughing and crying when reading slush, especially sci-fi because it often contained absolutely awful science. Her stories made him laugh too, and he subtlety mentioned his own attempts at a novel. Her response was exactly the opposite of what he expected. As they took the elevator back to their floor, she pestered him to let her read it, and explained that her publishing company was always looking for works with good science, and even more often for works that had cross-over potential between leisure reading and material that provides actual lessons.

Alan's book was accepted for publication in near-record time, and he moved onto a successful career as a writer of both sci-fi novels and science popularizations. If his timing had been just a little bit off that day, he might never have had the opportunity–or the encouragement– to risk that transition. Marissa became a weak tie that led to Alan's successful career change. Now imagine if Alan had been able to stay in touch with his weak ties, like Marissa, using social media. The infrastructure of social media makes it so much easier to maintain weak ties that it multiplies the openings for these serendipitous occasions that can be the make-or-break moment for anyone.

Six Degrees of Separation

Relationships with weak ties are responsible for the jobs we get, the opportunities and new knowledge that create innovation, and the resources we have access to. Because they operate in different social circles, they have information and knowledge that you–and probably most of your strong ties–don't have. Sticking to only your strong ties makes you susceptible to opportunity and information redundancy; you already know a lot of what your closest ties do. The different dimensions in which your weak ties operate span a huge range that you could never know by yourself. Staying within your close-knit groups of strong ties limits you from gaining the widespread knowledge from people who are busy doing very different things.

A weak tie might be a person who works in a related but separate industry, and who may know about jobs that you are qualified for but wouldn't otherwise be aware of. Like Marissa and Alan, these tangential connections open up a much wider range of opportunities. They are the source of interactions that can drive innovation through the novelty of ideas, and they come from unexpected directions. A merger of cross-disciplines has a better chance of generating something new. Moreover, the sheer number of weak ties equals a source of potential gain that you can't afford to ignore.

Social media is great at creating weak ties: you probably don't have as much intimacy and emotional investment in the wide range of people you connect with on Twitter, for example. The Internet is excellent for creating and maintaining this kind of connection. Better yet, empirical findings show that time online managing weak ties does not come at the expense of real-world relationships. Weak ties are where the currency of social capital gains value. Imagine if you found a very special penny. If you didn't know better, you would think it was only worth a cent–but to the right person, who understands and is interested in its uniqueness, that same penny could be worth tens of thousands of dollars. Strong and weak ties help to determine the ways you are able to exchange your currency–your social capital, and based on the content, your labor–for whatever you wish.

The Basis of Reciprocity

In many Eastern cultures, conventional wisdom dictates that you shouldn't stand out; there's the metaphor of the nail that gets beaten down because it stands above the rest. This philosophy may have changed some over the years, but in the United States, we tend to think of success in terms of individual achievements. Even in team settings, we invariably gravitate toward being individual stars.

The Me Paradox changes this, where the impact of relationships and exchange that helps everyone succeed together is what ultimately helps you succeed.

The Properties of Mutualism

Reciprocity is defined by social scientists as "the ongoing process of exchange with the aim of establishing and maintaining equality between parties."

Sounds relatively straightforward, right? That is until you dig a little deeper into its meaning. Ask yourself whether you think reciprocity is an ethical issue or a business practice. While you're considering that, think for a moment about the concept of reciprocity as the simplest mode of social business–one that underpins every exchange. We do it almost automatically through social norms and customs: when you say "Hi," I say "Hi" back.

The difficulties arise when you begin to value the items being exchanged. Is one person's "Hi" worth more than the other's? This is especially difficult with information, because the value of information is altered when it changes hands. There are times when reciprocity can be a kind of power exchange because an obligation is created. This is why we sometimes feel that we shouldn't accept a gift. It would be inappropriate and unethical to have even the possibility of an obligation between, say, a reporter and a politician.

Finding Common Ground

Equality and exchange affect the notion of reciprocity. Addressing the power position explicitly leads to building equality in relationships.

It is often easier for colleagues. Professionals, more often than not, are willing to take the first step when asked nicely to assist. For co-workers within an organization, it is part of an unwritten code of ethics. The knowledge management push of the 1980s was banking on this era where information and knowledge would be freely exchanged as part of a commodification effort that would break down the barriers of exchange by marginalizing the value of information. In many respects, the knowledge management push lacked momentum until the Internet came along.

Still, status tends to carry a lot of weight when exchanging information. These exchanges also have the dual purpose of showing or acquiring superiority. When conducting social business or allying with someone reputable, engage in altruistic behavior by giving first, but expect reciprocity on the basis of mutualism for stable, long-term exchanges. When reciprocation is denied and regard is absent, the exchange breaks down. Reciprocity is a signal of regard, and required to create social business relationships within the Me Paradox.

The Nature of Exchange

Exchange theory, at its very root, postulates that "individuals evaluate alternative courses of action in order to get the best value at the lowest cost from any transaction." As the definition implies, the approach is transactional; it treats everything, even interactions with people, as a one-time deal. The theory doesn't consider the notion of consequences or long-term implications. If a stock trader focuses only on one transaction and has no concern for the next, how successful would his tenure be on the floor of the New York Stock Exchange? How about a seller on eBay? The seller needs to be sure he gets the best return on his investment and, at the same time, satisfies the other party in order to receive positive feedback and reputation for future sales. Within social business, very little actually happens the way exchange theory would predict; the stock trader and the eBay seller, due to cultural norms or technical mechanisms, both use a variation of the exchange theory called the Social Exchange Theory.

Alternatively, social exchange theory takes a person out of the transactional mindset, and now the end goal is a long-term relationship. It is not as important to get every penny's worth of profit on this exchange if it means that you will not be able to make future exchanges. What you do today can be seen as an investment in future opportunities, and this happens through social business.

To get to the heart of social business requires the understanding and control of the goods and services as well as the impact of the exchange. People seek and form social business relationships in order to receive individual benefits that they do not believe can be acquired elsewhere–whether it is expertise, experience, services, or meaningful connections. Essentially, the key is to get the most out of the knowledge and information you have, while keeping others satisfied; in other words, you need to understand how business works when relationships, and not profits, are the goal.

BEST PRACTICE REVIEW

People join SBS because they want to be involved, to have the opportunity to trade and interact with other like-minded individuals; but the exchange itself is much more than the sum of its individuals.

On SBS, it helps to understand how others view you. This includes the ways reciprocity, mutualism, and social exchange impact their perception. Most SBS uses a combination of profile information and a reputation system to signify a user's status. A user's status can be affected not only by how they relate to other people in the real world, but also by how they conduct themselves online and within the professional network.

A variety of methods are employed to allow users to add positively or negatively to another user's personal status, thereby affecting how that user is perceived by the rest of the network. Rating another user can be carried out in a private or public manner. Having a positive status or testimonial is a type of trust mechanism, similar to the ratings system employed by eBay where auction transactions completed successfully or unsuccessfully are linked to a person's profile and will often determine whether another user will deal with them or not. This helps to explain why presence within SBS, as well as historical content within the context, provides valuable information that helps the user decide whether to trust another user. The emphasis now is not purely on association, but on merit and participation within the professional network itself.

Never have the days of peer review, group validation, and generally what others think of you been more important. Just another reason why, by operating under the Me Paradox–by concentrating on what you can do with and for others–you get more for yourself.

The Art of Exchange

Remember, the Me Paradox allows you to be extraordinary without taking more time out of your life; in fact, with social business, it will give you more time for recreation, family, leisure, etc. All you need is the desire and the ability to accept the risks and put behind you the fears of the unknown.

In social business, we need to be careful, we need to be prudent and finally, we need to take our time. A word to the wise: Never rush reputation building, no matter how badly you may want it. Pace yourself. The need for and use of patience is one of the many ways that exchange is more art than science.

When we select the appropriate networks to participate in, they help reduce the need to rush by creating barriers to entry. These barriers are inherent rules to a reputation system and the time it takes to learn and conform to the social or peer pressures that come about as a result of newly-formed associations. Moreover, when you find a couple networks and then build contacts before you need to exchange with them, you further reduce the need to rush. Obviously, traditional networking best practices apply also online, so do not wait until you need a network before you start building one. Spending time to get to know the other party is a critical signal that demonstrates your investment beyond the single transaction. Rushing reputation building hampers that signal.

Start immediately and build your coalition so that when the time comes, you will be able to engage in an exchange that is satisfying for both parties.

As we discussed earlier, your first, most crucial ally will be more altruistic than mutual. Best networking practices suggest that you have to give in order to get. Translation: prepare yourself to be altruistic in order to create the potential for long-term relationships that will be mutually beneficial. Research[8] indicates that generous individuals not only elicit higher rates of cooperation but also generate goodwill, the fuel that powers social business. It turns out that generosity, as a reputation trait, is sticky and spreads quickly, and this establishes trust and a positive reputation.

The Exchange Rate of Reputation

Once you find an appropriate social business site, the labor begins. Similar to the coalition-building cycle, almost anything you do online, or even offline, is considered labor. When you participate in SBS, this labor can be skillfully converted into currency, and currency is exchanged for all sorts of things.

The establishment of your reputation is directly correlated with how you go about generating this currency. If you are in it just for the single transaction, your reputation will reflect that. If you are working to build long-term relationships, your reputation will reflect that as well. But before we get into specific strategies, we should talk about the various types of currency that exist online.

Social Capital as Currency

The currency is social capital. Practically speaking, social capital refers to the connections both within your personal social network and among disparate social networks in your organization, at all levels– your department, group, division, partner network and alliances. As defined by Nahapiet and Ghoshal,[9] social capital is "the sum of the actual and potential resources embedded within, available through, and derived from the network of relationships possessed by an individual or social unit." Basically, this means the social capital is the trust, the culture of reciprocity, and the social networks someone or a group possesses. At its core, social capital means different things in various subject areas. It only recently has gained momentum in academia and business mindshare. And, like reputation, this intangible resource is connected to a gamut of benefits that are hard to measure and evaluate, and therefore usually ignored and classified as mere theory. Forming and maintaining relationships is a necessary precondition for the accumulation of social capital. You're more likely these days to hear businesses talking about social capital, which gives us indication that SBS have actual, tangible value. The great innovation at work within SBS is that they have taken what was once the murky realm of human relations and made them explicit and viewable by you, your coworkers, and your manager. What we commonly refer to as "networking" or "being connected" can now be monitored, measured, and quantified, which means that social capital can be cultivated and grown. This has already become big business, and a leading concern of forward-thinking CEOs and their human resource departments.

More Tangible than Ever Before

Social business has revitalized social capital where practices for harvesting and maintaining it have emerged. There are mountains of research in the mature field of Social Network Analysis (SNA), which shows that the quality of the networks have real implications on employee productivity and innovation. Network health, reach, density, and many other attributes have direct bearing on company and employee performance. Organizations might seek to develop social capital so that they can improve the performance of cross-functional groups, increase organization-wide collaboration, maximize the value of their strategic alliances and partner relations, boost the performance of managers, and improve supply chain dynamics.

University of Cincinnati Professor Mahyar Arefi suggested that organizations develop consensus quicker, and take collective action in their "shared interest" more readily as social capital is developed.

RESEARCH SUMMARY

What good is social capital? *Virtual Handshake* authors David Teten and Scott Allen[10] describe the following benefits to acquiring and using social capital:

• **Employment:** More people find jobs through personal contacts than by any other means.
• **Pay and promotion:** People with rich social capital are paid better and promoted faster at younger ages.
• **Influence and effectiveness:** People who are central in an organization's networks are more influential than those in the periphery.
• **Venture capital and financing:** Seventy-five percent of startups find and secure financing through the informal investing grapevine–the social networks of capital seekers and investors.
• **Organizational learning:** As much as 80 percent of learning in the workplace takes place through informal interactions.
• **Word-of-mouth marketing:** Traditional advertising increases awareness of products and services, but personal referrals and recommendations are extremely influential in the decision to purchase.
• **Strategic alliances:** The more strategic alliances a company creates, the more alliances it is likely to create in the future.
• **Financial stability:** Bankruptcy is less likely for firms with well-connected executives and board members, even when considering many other explanations.
• **Democracy:** In his 25-year study of democracy, Robert Putnam found that those regions in Italy with rich social capital enjoy stronger economic

development and more responsive local governments than regions with poor social capital.

• **Happiness:** Extensive studies in psychology and medicine have demonstrated that social capital improves personal quality of life, specifically, that a stronger social network leads to a greater sense of well being and meaning.

• **Health:** Putnam writes, "People who are socially disconnected are between two and five times more likely to die from all causes, compared with matched individuals who have ties." A high level of social capital is critical for your professional and personal success.

Social capital has been ignored for a long time because it is a form of implicit currency. Explicit currency is pretty obvious: it is tangible, like cash and gold. Implicit currency is intangible, conceptual, and harder to quantify. Social capital, a positive comment for instance, or a referral, a lead, a link, a positive rating, a kind word to an intermediary or in any way giving the gift of information, are considered implicit currency. With social business, status- or reputation-building contributions are also considered implicit currency.

We rarely think about how currency is used, especially cash and, to a higher degree, credit. There was a time when every U.S. dollar was backed by its equivalent weight in gold. This ensured that if anyone was unwilling to exchange it, the government would accept it. It built trust in the explicit currency system. Implicit currency also works when people trust its backing. The spine of social capital is reputation rather than gold.

The use of explicit currency is hard to exchange when creating ties to people you don't know well. Handing a one-hundred-dollar bill to a woman you just met normally doesn't always go over very well. Professionally, it signals an exaggerated attempt or over-zealous push to win favor, which most people are opposed to, especially in social business. The reciprocation rate is low and the risk for reputation damage is high.

Weak ties use social capital, or implicit currency, while strong ties use explicit currency, or tangible goods. In a Western culture, when presenting a person with tangible goods, the gift is typically wrapped and a price tag removed. Although most often the gift is expected to be unwrapped immediately after it is given and most often the relative price is known, it remains proper etiquette for exchanging explicit currency, even when there are strong ties. And, this is precisely why it is crucial to understand the role and use of implicit capital as we are primarily focused on developing weak ties.

Social Business Factor

Online reputation management helps explain how you can use and influence social capital at an individual level. It is not native or a byproduct of general Internet activity; you can't generate it just by surfing the Internet.

Social capital is earned through repeated exchanges, growth in networks, and the expansion and depth of trust with social business relationships. Although a direct correlation exists between partici-pation and the amount of social capital a person has, the quality of participation factors into the amount of social capital they generate. Be forewarned, hubris or exaggeration should not be used as a strategy to increase social capital. For instance, if you are not an expert, you should not go into a network 'guns blazing' and participating as if you are an expert and have this abundance of knowledge. This might satisfy a short-term goal, but it will be gained at the expense of generating more social capital. Rather, you should follow the natural upward path of the accumulation of social capital (the Long Tail), strategically participating when necessary and producing the highest yield possible. Don't let your social capital burn a hole in your pocket either. It does not necessarily need to be spent or used immediately. Think of it as credit you earn with a lender: as long as you keep your account open, you are able to access the line of credit anytime it's needed.

What Lies Ahead

We have all seen that there is value in relationships and reputation; however, one must practice the Me Paradox to reap those benefits. In consideration of the online reputation lifecycle, your presence is an investment, so others know about you and about what qualities you bring, and how you will cooperate and reciprocate. In the process of finding the right networks and participating to build up a social business relationship, your engagement in the network, and how much social capital you build up depends on how you present yourself, and this is manifested as your online reputation.

In the next chapter, we will explore what factors motivate one to codify and share knowledge that benefits others. We will also examine a few traditional networking best practices that may play a critical role in your engagement strategy, which I will explain in detail in **Chapter 9**.

~chapter eight~
The Science of Engagement

The real world and the online world are becoming more integrated daily as they converge with devices like the iPhone and through technologies like **geotagging**. Think about it, almost every person over the age of 12 has a cell phone and most homes have internet access. More and more of us are not even getting around without GPS technology these days. As these technologies and the popularity of social media continue to grow over the next decade, there are likely to be far-reaching implications. Based on what we know so far and the rapid pace of changes in technology, the best we can get is a glimpse into what lies in store.

Consider the following scenario: You are sitting at a bar, a restaurant, or a charity event, and through geocoding, you know who is in the room, what their backgrounds are, and whether or not you are connected to them in some way. On your handheld device, and with just the tap of a screen, you pull up their online reputation and now you know a bit more about who they are–you might even get a quick introduction by a mutual contact if they are also in the room with you. Now consider this: If everyone is networked and you are not, what opportunity was missed? Are you now the anonymous 'nobody' in the room? Your dream job could have been within your grasp and you didn't even know it.

That might sound harsh, but it's the reality in the today's workplace. We are seeing a shift from individuals–who depend on social relations dominated by locally embedded, unmediated, given and stable relations–into networked individuals, who are more dependent on their own combination of strong and weak ties, their personal network. These individuals switch networks, cross boundaries, and weave their own web of instrumental and relatively fluid relationships. This modern enterprise on the horizon is social business. And, like it or not, it is the wave of the future. Products are too complex for one individual, the landscape is too volatile for a small group to manage, and economies are too dynamic for an isolated firm to survive. As you can see, the Me Paradox is not only interesting, but it will soon be necessary for survival.

Organic Design of Relationships

Successful social business professionals are taking advantage of emergence as a concept. Suppose a new college green area is going to be opened up at SMU (Social Media University). Where should the flagstone pathways through the grass be placed? A landscape architect might use a classical design, or presume to know in advance the pathways that students will use. But the SMU gardeners defer the decision of where to place the pathways until the students have worn a path in the grass, and only then do they place the flagstones.

If they had chosen the wrong area, the students would have ignored the stones, and created the optimal dirt paths anyway, marring the aesthetics. But by deferring the organization and letting the pathway design emerge, they let the users produce the optimal result. Although a landscape architect could have produced a beautiful design on paper, the gardeners knew from experience that the best use would evolve by letting the pathways emerge from patterns of use over time. Successful web, content, and information designers today employ emergence to produce better results than they have been able to in the past, and thus become more like gardeners who refuse to dictate, and instead cultivate beauty, design, and information from natural sources; the essential mindset of a Me Paradox practitioner.

The Analysis of Social Business

The social business equivalent of watching students wear in their own pathways is the way analysts are observing the patterns emerging from people's natural social networks, and it is called Social Network Analysis (SNA). J.L. Moreno, the father of sociometry, which studies interpersonal relations, conducted a groundbreaking experiment in a reform-school dormitory where each resident would decide who they considered a friend and whether that person reciprocated or not. His goal was to allow rapport and social ties to determine who roomed with whom by finding people who enjoyed each others' company or complemented each others' skills. In figure 8-1, what looks like a densely packed spider web is actually a depiction of relationships, a graphical representation of a social network that can be traced by SNA. By studying the resulting web of interconnections, Moreno created a whole new field of study.

Figure 8-1
_____

SOCIAL NETWORK ANALYSIS GRAPH

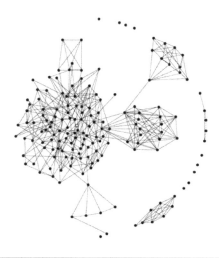

_____

SNA is quantifiable and lists a growing suite of applications. The analysts are able to examine patterns of interactions and gain a better understanding of business outcomes, such as job performance, job satisfaction, adoption of new ideas or technologies, knowledge transfer, and innovation. The programs that perform SNA, like others in the same vertical, are getting more advanced everyday. They consist of four parts: network definition, network manipulation, structural features, and visual inspection. The technology may seem complex, but its use is simple in its identification of where the relationships lie, how the information flows, and the connectedness of an organization or group.

Some thought leaders have expressed concern that if employees get hold of Social Network Analysis (SNA), they will use it to advance their own careers, rather than acting for the benefit of the company. In all reality, this is unlikely. The new technologies favor openness, sharing, and connectedness, and only those who participate to the fullest extent will stand out from the crowd. Improving the quality and reach of your network will certainly advance careers, and employers stand to benefit from the effort. At the same time, the occasional employee will learn to game the system the way they game other indiscriminately applied measurements of employee performance. As The Social Capital Foundation points out, we shouldn't be overly concerned with the manifestations of social capital, such as the number of friends in your network, or the number of discussion posts and comments a person makes. We've all known windbags in our careers, people who are, as Shakespeare would have categorized, "full of sound and fury signifying nothing." It's true that SBS gives them more of a platform from which to blow. Even though it may take more careful analysis, trusted networks can weed even them out. It is "the disposition to create, maintain and develop such networks that constitutes real social capital."[1] And ultimately, that disposition shines through in those that rise to the top. This sort of connection quality has a lot to do with the quality of your personal network. We know intuitively that a connection with your VP can be worth more to your career or your company than your connection with your buddy Frank in the cubicle down the hall, who rants about the economy and government policies. SNA can help quantify that value on a massive scale.

Applied Science

Who has the information and how is it being propagated? Executives and strategists use SNA reports to show how to improve their organization from a tacit knowledge dimension. As this science hits the mainstream, information-hoarding or 'flying under the radar' will be a signal of bottleneck, and it will be dealt with. Not participating is a beacon, a red flashing light blinking in the face of the decision makers of your organization. SNA is the future. It is a viable tool, as studies have shown, and we can all benefit from its practical guidance. Of all the things that should entice you as the archetype, this should be the most significant reason to learn how to engage in social business. SNA fills in the gaps of peer reviews and cohesion reports about your activity and creates a holistic view of YOU.

In late 2008, Forrester, as part of the Talent Management Research Practice, conducted a broad and comprehensive survey of highly ranked human resource managers and directors working for the top 500 global firms. Within the report, analyst Zach Thomas showed that although they ranked the analyses as "above average" or "extremely" important, less than half felt they were capable of making a clear decision on whom to retain, promote, or fire. This is because human resource managers and directors are too disconnected from individuals in large companies. Even with the processes and tools available today, we still struggle to measure performance and an individual's value to an organization. There is a fine line between what you achieve, what you deserve, and what you gain. SNA, and social business in general, is moving to improve this aspect.

These tools also help better recognize the stars–people who are doing something way beyond what they are required to do–turning what some see as a disadvantage into an advantage. SNA gives management the ability to see who has connections with whom, who is not connected, who chose whom, the reciprocal nature of relationships, and how strong or weak those ties are. These bonds, or lack thereof, separate the information hubs from the information hoarders, especially in regard to tacit knowledge. Creating and maintaining your online presence and reputation is only going to become more important with these advances on the horizon. The social business movement is so broad that tools, technologies, and even processes are being dragged along with it.

Analyzing Perception

Understanding how participants perceive other participants, both formally and informally, is the key to creating and utilizing a connection. The signals sent–the participation style, the language used, the reputation (network and web)–will play an important role in determining whether the opportunity at hand will unfold or be discarded. Engagement and engagement phase strategy are really about the awareness of the signals you send and how they come across to your connections. This is of paramount importance in determining the future route and successful undertaking of this enterprise.

Critical Signals and Their Meanings

Signaling theory was developed to explain what keeps communication honest. In LinkedIN, for example, having connections, and especially having those connections verify or recommend you, is a highly reliable signal, as many executive recruiters have stated. There is a heavy cost in loss of reputation for anyone who falsifies information.

There are many reasons for deceptive behavior in social networks. Beyond the tangible gains, there are indirect gains, such as appearing to be popular, important, or an expert. Sorting out the truth by understanding different signals is a key skill for online communicators. Some signals have qualities that make them much more reliable than others: the basic rule of thumb is that for a signal to be reliable, the consequences of producing a fake signal must outweigh the benefits.

Unlike conventional signals, assessment signals are difficult to fake because the cost for sending a fake signal is imposed by something external and reliable. Researcher Judy Donath, in her study *Signaling in Social Supernets,*[2] describes assessment signals as inherently reliable, "because producing the signal requires possessing the indicated quality. Lifting a 500-pound weight is a reliable signal of strength; a weaker person simply cannot do it." There are also assessment signals that function as "strategic" or "handicap" signals. Sending these signals may seem to be a disadvantage to the signaler, but it's actually a way of showing that she can afford the cost because she has so much of a given resource. A peacock's tail takes a tremendous amount of energy to maintain; a peacock shows his biological adaptation by being able to spend that energy on a display, a signal.

Some costs involve social norms and expectations. Donath characterizes these as conventional signals, where:

> [T]he link between signal and quality is arbitrary, a matter of social convention. ... Conventional signals are kept honest through the outside intervention of laws and social mores. A siren on a car is a conventional signal of being an official emergency responder. Anyone can buy one and use it to speed through traffic, but society imposes costs on those who do so illegitimately.

Signals can be evaluated by determining whether the cost of deception is low. If it is, the reliability of the signal is low as well. Donath points out that "self-descriptions in online profiles are mostly conventional signals—it is just as easy to type 24 or 62 as it is to enter one's actual age, or to put M rather than F as one's gender." If the community isn't vigilant about imposing costs for people who don't meet conventions, then conventional signals are nearly meaningless.

A Collaborative Effort

Signaling is where the network–the community involved–becomes critical. Since a large majority of the signaling that occurs online is conventional, the signals are less reliable. The network provides meaning to the signals because honesty is enforced by other members of the community. In the LinkedIN example above, it is connections verifying connections and making recommendations; other members of the community are enforcing honesty.

This process of mutual verification brings to surface reasons why choosing the right network matters. LinkedIN is made up specifically of business professionals sharing business information, so they set a standard that is appropriately high: the information has to be very accurate. But what about, say, the profile page of an online gamer in a fantasy gaming community? Donath writes, "Putting one's profile in a social network site, linked to by one's acquaintances, places it into a context subject to the latter's social mores, be they for factual truthfulness or identity play," and that mutual verification means descriptions are true, although it is important to note that "true" means "true to the mores of our community," which can range from strict adherence to known facts to highly imaginative role-playing.

Professional Signals

Social capital is highly context-dependent; meaning it's bound by the network or group in which it was created. So engaging in a network where you can't get what you want doesn't ultimately produce much value. Distinguishing between networks that foster social business and those that don't is incredibly difficult because the value of social capital is often unknown; social capital doesn't accrue in an account with a neat ledger book and running balance.

As a result, while you work on finding the right networks to fit your goals, keep in mind that a social business professional should convey at least three signals along the way: (1) You are confident and able to express your thoughts (competent); (2) you are comfortable in the medium and understand the value of participation (predictable); (3) and you are passionate enough about your work and your career to become proactive and put the effort into your online reputation (reliable). These three signals, and the ability to send them authentically, maximizes the transferability of social capital from one network to another, which makes them well worth cultivating.

Integrating into the Network

Engagement, or more specifically, networking involves building a group or system of interconnected people within the network who exchange information, contacts, and experiences for professional purposes or social business. Everything we put online is part of our engagement strategy, so we need to make sure it conforms to the principles of the signaling theory. Online, much of what people want to know about other people is not directly observable, so we rely on signals. There are particular ways that humans use signals to create, use, and enforce authenticity. Understanding how those signals operate, along with the tactics to accurately convey them, give you an edge in the networking effort.

Principles of Negotiation

The intricacies of signaling require you to pay attention to more than the explicit features of your communication and networking. It takes specific skills, such as negotiation, to be aware of and manage those rarely taught, implicit aspects of your participation. An understanding of some fundamental negotiation principles ensures your activities accurately match your intentions. Use the negotiation principles that follow as a relationship framework to establish and emphasize the authenticity of your signals.

Negotiation is the art of creating cooperation in spite of *seemingly* dissimilar interests. The principles of negotiation are not dependent on the identity of the parties involved, their cultures, or the item(s) at stake. The skill of negotiation can be applied universally—whether seeking help, fundraising, buying a used car from eBay, or developing an online relationship. Renowned author and negotiator Dennis Ross[3] sets out just how much value there is in understanding how to arrive at a practical and pragmatic negotiation strategy, whether in politics or in business.

In any negotiation, it's key to know two things going in: what you want, and what you can live without. And keep in mind the Me Paradox: it's not all about you. When the stakes are high, each party has an abstract idea of what they want, but hasn't thought through the bottom line of what is acceptable. This is where things get tricky. If you have no idea what you want, your potential contact will create a vision that serves him or her.

It helps to think things through ahead of time. For instance, you may want every contact to become an enthusiastic supporter of your content published online, but does that mean that they will refer others to you, or just include you on their friends list? Even if it's just having a weak tie that you can use in the future, knowing your intended result is the first step to achieving your intended result.

Almost as important as knowing yourself is knowing everything there is to know about the other side of the negotiation. While it's largely impossible to have perfect knowledge of what you're up against in any negotiation, Ross contends that it's important to know three things:

- What their motivations are?
- Where the influence lies on their side?
- What they need to take from the encounter?

It also helps, he says, to have an appreciation of the external forces or pressures that might affect their position. How is their industry dealing with the recent economic downturn? Who in the network influences them? It's not a negotiation if you can't offer something beneficial to the other side. Knowing what they view as valuable means that you are prepared to engage in social business.

Once you know what's important to both sides, you can start to build a relationship of trust with the potential contact.

Start by conducting your own research and get a sense of the territory/network you will be dealing in. Do you share a common audience? Trust is built when you establish your credibility by making an effort to listen and understand your potential contact's needs and concerns. By listening actively, you are laying a foundation for the potential contact to listen to you in response. Communication, or engagement, makes cooperation possible.

This understanding of the other side isn't some secret weapon to be concealed. In order to gain the most social capital possible, you must prove you understand what is important to the potential contact. The quickest path to failure occurs when an individual just comes out and states his or her needs, without showing any understanding or concern for the needs or wants of the other side. This intuitive knowing of the needs of the other side demonstrates that you are working with them, and not against them. Neither side is in a negotiation in order to be altruistic. Cooperate in the spirit of mutualism and you can start the positive feedback loop of cooperation. Negotiation is the art of creating cooperation. Know yourself, know your audience, and engage to create cooperation.

We're a Human Network

You have picked the right networks and you understand the power of signaling and negotiation. No matter how prepared and skilled you are, you should always expect to make mistakes. Don't let the fear of failure be a reason to not take the plunge. Now is the time to push away that fear and take this opportunity to build a strong network. Your personal network should be based on good choices about whom to connect with and what behaviors you use; these parts of your network exemplify who we are and who we want to be. There is no rush to take everyone on as your friend, especially considering the risky behaviors of a few, so concentrate on connecting with people who have similar values and interests and those who understand the implications of your online reputation.

Remember, someday, everyone will have some sort of blemish on their record as we're all only human. Everyone is imperfect. A robust character is not about perfection, but the constant pursuit of it. Trust in yourself and your abilities. Be pragmatic, but let passion and intuition lead the way, not the fear of failure.

People Sensemaking

In 2002, Millen and Patterson[4] coined the term "People Sensemaking." Its definition is not elusive. Just as it sounds, *people sensemaking* involves making sense of who people are using only context. The term was created to mainly apply to what is happening online, especially as we explore different social networks. According to their paper, people sensemaking is the process a person goes through to gain a general understanding or gist of a person and their role in a network or online community.

To get a better feel of what sensemaking is in general, let's imagine that we are driving over a mountain summit pass in the heart of winter. As we ascend the mountain and there is snow all around, we almost do not know what to expect, especially if this is a new experience. Our sensemaking abilities organize the chaos around us as we adapt to our environment and the situation. As we continue climbing and gain altitude on the mountain, we become acutely aware of the higher elevation and the poor visibility while we continue to climb, challenged by the ice and snow.

We create mental models as we slow down, grip the steering wheel with two hands, and begin to ask ourselves questions: Do I need snow chains? Should I turn around? Should I stop and wait the storm out? It almost seems like instinct. It is categorized, socially defined, and then labeled as a bad situation. We think we are using deductive reasoning to evaluate and decide our next course of action. In fact, we may test our presumption of the environment. The determining factor is based on what we have learned and picked up from our experiences. This is not a question of logic, but of social context discovery.

We look to each other, human to human, traveler to traveler, employee to employee, to make sense of a phenomenon. You may not understand everything that is going on in the driving analogy, especially if you have never driven over a mountain pass during the winter. This analogy really is about watching the environment. The environment in your network is made up of people. You need to make sense of who they are according to what you have learned, your experiences, and your attitudes. The point is that oftentimes, whom you watch and whom you follow determines what you are going to do and ultimately, who you are going to be.

Those you select to engage with is important. Mimicking influencers, being in communion with leaders of a group or industry, is not only desired, but warranted as you select and then join their groups. Don't be afraid to mimic their personality, so to speak, and learn to make sense of your environment and the people around you through the eyes of the influencer and the people you are intertwined with. Their ways may be foreign or strange at times, but they are experienced and know how to navigate the sometimes icy terrain.

Adaptive Unconscious

Of course, it is possible to have too much information. The shear amount of people in a network and the information about them can cause a sort of overload that could lead to rash decisions. There has been a recent blast of research that leads us to believe our experiences reach us at our unconscious core and help us develop our inner voice. Malcom Gladwell, in his 2003 book *Blink,*[5] indicates that sometimes too much information is more harmful than good. Too much research causes the brain to overload and then not work as effectively. His entire book speaks to the underlying human mechanism called the adaptive unconscious–things we do and feel without actively knowing about them. He provides numerous examples as to why a logic malfunction can occur when reading from multiple, credible sources like CNN and NY Times.

If this doesn't ring a bell, have you ever tried shopping for a car, or a home appliance, and after so many models, options, colors, etc., you ended up making a rash decision…the process and the information overload tired or frustrated you and you made an impulse buy? What is happening is that our brains can only compute so much, and with the enormous proliferation of information literally at our finger tips, we shut off. We try to learn so much so quickly that our brains subconsciously gives-up and says, "Who cares, this is not that important... What a big waste of time and energy. ..." This is precisely why major high-powered executives like the famed Jack Welch of GE ask for a one-pager of the situation or summary. He doesn't need the manual or a detailed description explaining the reasoning behind why something will work. He trusts his sources and his ability, so he only needs a synopsis.

RESEARCH SUMMARY

In the late '70s Weston Agor noted far before the likes of John Naisbitt and Malcolm Gladwell that intuition is more than an emotional response. It is an actual skill that can be learned and developed. However, our ability to intelligently intuit has become diluted and mystified, leading many pundits to discredit it, placing it back in the realm of fantasy. Ken Paller, professor of psychology at Northwestern University and intuition researcher, conducted experiments that showed that parts of our brain light up when our sub-conscious mind is working, leading us to believe that we might remember things that we are not aware of. In a 2009 research study, he demonstrates the brain activity of people when they are seemingly occupied or not paying attention. His research showed that in certain situations the subject did better recalling patterns when not trying to memorize them. In essence, we are better equipped when we don't think too hard, we don't try too much, or we don't rack our brains trying to figure out difficult-to-understand people, their behaviors, problems, and situations. Related research demonstrates people's behavior in making snap decisions, which considers another form of our adaptive unconscious. By tracking eye movements, UK researchers[6] found that we have trouble making good decisions when we have too much information. This is because our conscious mind tries to put patterns, categorize, and make everything logical. In fact, researchers found that the old cliché 'first thought, best thought', may hold some water as those who had no time to think made better decisions. Our unconscious self does a better job of making decisions when decisions are complex or about complex things that have multiple options and attributes to consider.

Intuitive Networking

Peel away the onion and you will find that many people who use their intuition have also had great experiences. Your reputation, your weak ties (personal network), the networks you belong to, your job, and everything we have taken stock of is basically about your own unique experiences. Consolidating these experiences into useful information is like what a Barista does with a perfectly brewed cup of Espresso. Only the finest amount, tiny in comparison, is produced in a cup of Espresso. That is very akin to the secret sauce of social business success. Funnel all the richness from sources that you trust into a tiny cup of information that you use to make a decision. Achieve this and you will achieve social business success. This truism applies equally to everyone, regardless of their situation. And, when combined with the Me Paradox, that my friends, is the perfect brew.

Find the balance and you will have the key to open many different doors to worlds of opportunity and fortune. But don't make the mistake of thinking that intuition can replace hard work. Research[7] has shown that conscious thought is optimal for making tough decisions, including whether to buy a certain house or make an investment choice. But in cases of random events and complex things like people's behavior, whom you trust, whom you engage with, and whom you build relationships with, intuition trumps good old fashioned conscious thought.

The Pot of Gold

Once established, amazing things can be done with a personal network. A recent example is the role social media and the Internet played in President Barack Obama's election campaign. Already widely recognized as a social networking case study in 21st-century marketing, the Obama campaign's media strategy was a key factor in the president's ability to gain a significant monetary advantage over the well-funded Hillary Clinton, and then John McCain. The advantage was even more remarkable because so much of it came from hundreds of thousands of small donations collected from his website–the Long Tail. In 2007, Obama said 258,000 people had already donated money to his campaign. By July 2008, this trend had accelerated to the point that in that month alone he collected $51 million from 65,000 donors. In the last four months of the campaign, he outspent John McCain by $100 million dollars, which he used primarily on TV ads in key battleground states.[8] According to *AdWeek*, "Obama outspent McCain at a rate of 10-to-1" using email, mobile applications, his web site, Facebook, and even video game ads. He spent $2.8 million per day in August 2008 on online ads. The new and old media expenditures that experts largely credit in deciding the election would not have been possible without this new media strategy. The campaign used social media not just to raise money, but to energize, inform, solidify, leverage, and at crucial moments, mobilize a network of Obama supporters to volunteer locally, call their neighbors, and hold meetings, all basically channeling the Me Paradox.

Creating Your Network

A personal network with impact is far too important for your business success to ignore. In its simplest form, networking is about getting to know new people. There is a lot of information about networking in general, and a growing amount of information available about professional networking online. But simply working within the Me Paradox to adopt the right attitude and remain focused on the individual goals you have set for yourself-these may include developing your image and reaching your goals of how many contacts or connections you will build-ensures the digital footprint you leave will continually deliver positive results, even in the long run.

BEST PRACTICE REVIEW

Your personal network's value is contained largely in the weak ties within it. The strategy here is to practice the Me Paradox with the entire network. By focusing on the larger group, efficiently using the available tools to maintain your weak tie network, you develop the option to initiate deeper and stronger contacts when required.

These tools, inherent in SBS, include implicit relationship links, social bookmarking, tag clouds, wikis, and blogs. For instance, social bookmarking can reveal patterns, identify the interests or expertise of different individuals, or simply act as a repository of trusted pointers to other sources of information. Likes and dislikes (also referred to as taste sharing) are a general mechanism that can be used to aggregate opinions. It may also be used in the same way as social bookmarking, but in other contexts. Social tagging uses metadata, or labels supplied by users, and through folksonomies, these create more useful and natural classification schemes than any top-down approach. Content rating and reputation management occur when participants rate other participants or content. These examples help drive recommendations and relevancy, as well as reinforce the good, while suppressing the trivial or irrelevant–leaving only the finest amounts.

Online Reputation Management

Whether or not we realize it, we all live and work in a networked world. Networking is the new work. As a result, reputations matter. Relationships matter.

Engagement is the final component of the online reputation lifecycle. It is also the most intangible and often has negative connotations: you can't quantify it, it's highly variable, and often seen more as philosophy than science. Your participation has indirect and sometimes direct consequences. The details of online engagement are subjective, context-driven, and at times random because engagement deals with people. Think of it like a game of blackjack. Some people believe it a game of pure luck. Yet those with a certain amount of awareness and strategy (simply playing the odds consistently) seem to result in better gains than playing on the luck theorem. You've been dealt into the game of relationships already–wouldn't you like to know how best to play the cards you've got?

Playing Your Hand

You may not have asked to be in this game, but like it or not, social business is how organizations get things done today. Learning how to interact, negotiate, and cooperate with others is the only way to survive and thrive in this the new world. The outdated paradigms of industrialization where standardization, specialization, hierarchy, and command-and-control are being replaced with dynamic, diversified, and flat entrepreneurial systems. We now live in an interdependent world–the Economy of Regard.

London Business School professor Gary Hamel wrote in the *Harvard Business Review*[9] that we need "daring goals that will motivate a search for radical new ways of mobilizing and organizing human capabilities." It is important to act soon since traditional hierarchies are being replaced by more 'natural' hierarchies where status and influence are defined by participation rather than position.

Having job security or career success should not be ceilinged by something so basic as our capacity to network or our ability to engage with others. We should not have to change our nature, act like someone we are not, in order to succeed. And we don't. The Me Paradox is centered on this concept.

But a reputation could not be earned or used without people. So in the next chapter, an emphasis is placed on understanding the game and playing with a strategy in order to give us an advantage and allow us to achieve our goals without changing our basic nature.

~chapter nine~
Online Engagement

You are part of an information revolution that is changing the way people find and consume information. More than ever before, we are affecting information flow. Yet we are so busy that many times we do not stop and reflect on how we take part in these ongoing changes.

Seemingly contradictory to this notion is the fact that people are becoming less dependent on others for information. In this age, direct involvement with others is not always necessary. "Just Google it" is a household phrase. We no longer run to a doctor to help diagnose a discomfort or pain; we simply search for its symptoms and self-diagnose. We don't need a car salesman to tell us all the features of the latest model car; we Google it and do our own research.

But even when we trust the online source, people are still necessary to make the process work for us. We want to test drive the car before we buy it. If we're sick, we still need a doctor to prescribe a remedy.

Since we are not medical practitioners, we need others to mediate the information we find on the web through either application or dialogue. This promotes better comprehension. You wouldn't feel comfortable with non-medical personnel reading from Web MD and diagnosing you during an office visit, for example.

So the issue is not necessarily information, but rather knowledge, and since knowledge does not readily transport, we need people to help us put it in the context from which it was generated.

For knowledge transfer to be successful, both parties need to get involved. Information is more useful when it flows both ways. And in order to trust in the reliability of the information we need to know something about the expertise behind the advice.

A level of trust is central to many agencies and systems. City permit departments, a state approval board for contractors, or even the Better Business Bureau. These agencies and systems exist to build consumer trust.

The same theory is in operation online. Web MD can't take individual circumstances into account, but users can add to the equation, generating content while helping each other describe similar symptoms and so on. When a doctor chimes in, it becomes much more valuable. Knowing who is mediating the information is, at times, as important as the information itself.

Information is not knowledge, but with the amount of information and access we have at our finger tips, some of us tend to think we are experts at car shopping, buying real estate, using social media, you name it. Without a doubt, information makes us more informed. And in the hands of smart capable people, it can be highly effective. But those who dedicate countless hours and days studying and practicing in their area of expertise add immense value to information, transforming it into knowledge, and in some cases, wisdom.

We are living in a time of social isolation and, as technology advances, the trend will continue. Since we require less human contact to get information and to get by on a day-to-day basis, personal networks have become more important. These networks are new forms of relationships. Distances no longer separate us, so the local friendships and relationships (ties bound by proximity) we once required are no longer critical to survival.

This gives way to a societal transformation whereby people who have never met in person exchange information and favors as part of a new social economy. The personal networks and our need to understand who is mediating the information are racing toward each other; the engagement phase is at the finish line. It is where the culmination of your efforts in the prior two phases are finally actualized. But keep in mind, this imaginary finish line continues to move, just as rapidly as the technology changes.

Keep Up with the Pack

A lot of us don't look at the Internet as a competitive advantage. After all, most everyone in this day and age, has relatively the same access to it. But when we start to realize how to utilize the relationships and connections available to us, information is transformed into something much more valuable.

This is where the competitive advantage comes into play. The types of engagement activities are plentiful: share, link, tag, organize, barter, pitch, and publish. As we participate in all of these activities, we need engagement tactics as a way to authentically and systematically communicate across our network. The reason is best summarized with one word: CHANGE. Networks change over time. Just think about Facebook, MySpace, Twitter, and now your corporate network. Technology changes how we interact; or it changes the dynamics of human relationships online. As human beings, we have perceptions, thoughts, and personalities that change with the context. And events, such as the global economy, media, and government activities make the world we live in fluid and dynamic.

It is not happenstance when leaders read about other leaders. It is no mistake when people religiously follow certain blogs and track every Tweet. There are so many people who have incredibly diverse insights. The number of connections available to us provides us with near infinite possibilities.

By modifying a few activities you do in a day and then socializing the output of those activities, you create an accelerated system of learning and relationship building. Reflectively, weak ties and the groups within SBS both act as a buffering layer. The rapid explosion in technologies has made what is happening in cyberspace and beyond chaotic. Smartphones, Bluetooth, iPads, portable devices, web search engines, gated SBS, and the list continues to grow while our ability to manage this vast sea of information lessens each day. We must look to our network, our personal connections, to filter the desired information and provide the most relevant insights.

The Social Business Professional

Clout counts. Just look at any corporation and watch how executives are recruited and on-boarded. Typically they walk in the door with a certain amount of clout already established. That trusted position is necessary to allocate and motivate resources. So, ask yourself: Would I be more effective if people knew me already? What could I achieve? The sky truly is the limit if we put forth the effort to develop our reputation.

Developing our online reputation allows us to have that slice of power as we enter into new professional environments. How many times have you Googled the new executive or employee on your team? Next time you start a job or join a new project team, those who do Google you will recognize the influence you have already developed through their review of your online reputation.

It is when we want to remain unknown in this new era that the problems set in. As social business matures online and in the workplace, not being known increases the likelihood of not getting the job. Furthermore, assimilation into the work environment becomes more of a challenge as the mechanisms of group integration have gone social. If he wants to succeed, the social business professional must learn and adapt to operating professionally on the social web and using his online reputation accordingly.

The foundation of the engagement strategy balances objectives with sound practices. Networks require voluntary participation and, as you now know, are founded on the principle of reciprocity. However, there are two principles to internalize prior to starting any engagement activity. They are described here:

- Context awareness–this includes conversation types and the level of group cohesiveness or intimacy.
- e-Professionalism–this means net etiquette by the way of professional signals coupled with information fashion.

Beneficial Group Think

Humans tend to coalesce into small units; groups, communities, cliques, or networks hold great potential. These are the gatekeepers to success and development, and without them, the benefits and career potentials are much harder to achieve.

Group dynamics are broadly defined using many concepts. To earn a business degree in the United States, an organizational behavior course is required to help students understand this dynamic. But as we all know, this dynamic is going digital. So while colleges are only beginning to offer classes in subjects such as "virtual teams," the group-forming dynamics are rapidly changing. Learning how to integrate with groups in a virtual space will be a survival requirement for the social business professional.

Conversation Types

The perception of online group dynamics is often focused on technology, such as instant messenger or discussion forums. But don't be deceived. These elements only surround and support the core motivation for them: conversation. In a professional environment, group dynamics are centered on the types of conversations that exist. Figure 9-1 is an adaptation of an image used by Sean O'Driscoll, an ex-Microsoft Community Manager,[1] now working as an independent Social Business consultant.

Figure 9-1

WHEEL OF CONVERSATIONS

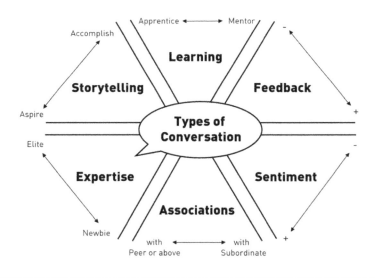

Each activity on the perimeter of the circle is a way to understand conversations and evaluate the environment.

For instance, if everyone is giving each other 'feedback' and 'storytelling', a possible mentorship exists. This is akin to a mentorship-centric network and in contrast to an environment where all the conversations are about 'expertise'.

In an expertise-driven network, every member is expected to contribute to the knowledgebase, and anyone not able to do this would eventually be ostracized and considered a resource drain. Mentorship would be out of place here.

But keep in mind that these conversation types are not mutually exclusive. Many networks have one or more types. Knowing which types of conversations are taking place, even at a sub-group level, will give you an advantage; it pertains to your understanding of what is appropriate and what is not.

Generally in larger networks, those who are to the relative right of each relational activity (see figure 9-1) are generating social capital, and those to the left are spending it. For example, in a storytelling conversation, Jose may tell a story about a recent accomplishment–maybe a large deal or a project completed within budget and on time. He provides details as to how he **accomplished** this feat. Jose's story is a contribution to the group, so he is generating social capital.

Now on the flip side of that conversation, think about Mohan who drones on about his preparation for the Project Management Professional test. While talking about these **aspirations**, he is using social capital within the group dynamic by subconsciously soliciting feedback. If users choose to reciprocate, it will only be to earn social capital or because they feel obligated according to social norms. Most people will be cordial, but the interaction isn't helping Mohan's reputation. In the grand scheme, social capital functions similar to that of credit cards with payments, balances, and limits, and when maxed out, holders like Mohan will be viewed as a drain on the group.

Conversations reveal writing styles, demeanor, etiquette, group culture, and most relevant of all, the relationship between the conversers, particularly those who carry a positive social capital balance.

An encouraging reply, helpful information, tips, and support can go a long way in the right network. Those who begin this process with the tools they have been provided here will begin to identify with the most influential members–those most likely mediating the information.

Social capital is intangible, so it is important to accurately gauge the different conversation types and where they fall within the spectrum. Think of yourself as an investigator, not a casual observer. You want to evaluate conversations before engaging, then transform your observations into a tactic for integration.

Level of Intimacy

Generating social capital is a great way to integrate into the group as long as it meets the group's and your own acceptable level of intimacy.

Relationships built online range from low to heavy investments and from weak to strong ties. Mutual trust is paramount to developing a relationship. Trust, for all intents and purposes, is the willingness to take on risk from an exchange with a contact. Sometimes SBS features help enable this trust and sometimes this falls solely on the group. Even when enabled by technology, trust is a matter of understanding and meeting the level of intimacy between parties.

This is a forerunner to putting into play our negotiation tactics–learning everything we can about the opposing side, especially who they are and what they want.

From a group integration standpoint, we are at an advantage because we have the ability to research and then decide whom we want to deal with. The bullets below are all critical but perhaps even more importantly, one must first identify the influential members in the group and work to ally with them.

In order to achieve group integration success, we need to also consider:

- The group as a whole
- The state of the media involved (that is, the tools or SBS features used)
- Subject matter and/or conversation type

When we interact with people offline, we tend to use our instincts more and react depending on our alignment with others. Online or virtually, we should spend considerable time researching and selecting where we interact and whom we interact with, but that isn't always the case.

When we finally do engage online, we adapt either by topic or by the context of the situation. So as we try to build our reputation and integrate into a group, we need a better understanding of what we are comfortable with, as well as the level of intimacy of the group and the people we want to engage with.

Use the following assessment to help you rate and understand your personal comfort levels and interests within a group setting. Score each hint accordingly, so that you can match the level of intimacy to your comfort. This is an important prerequisite to creating relationships; thus, it is helpful when integrating with the group. Understanding your own comfort zone and interests will also allow you to remain consistent. Remember, consistency is a core premise of reputation and, as we know, everything is hinged here.

INTIMACY ASSESSMENT

On a scale of 1 to 5, rate how comfortable you are with the described interaction, with 1 being "very uncomfortable or little interest" and 5 being "very interested or most comfortable." Remember to rate your preferences according to your comfort level with interactions within a group setting only. This does not apply to how you feel with close family members and friends.

Information-Gathering
Interaction that entails joining others to gather, to discuss, or to share information that is relevant to a person or group. Examples include topic- or context-driven searches where participants openly add to the knowledgebase.

_____

Humor
Interaction designed to get others to laugh or to display the sense of humor of the group. Examples include jokes, sarcasm, ability to laugh at oneself, etc. _____

Shared Activities
Interaction that involves doing things together with the group or a potential contact, but with the initiator making the decision about "what to do." Examples include volunteering, assistance, and attending face-to-face events. _____

Initiation
Interaction that involves taking charge and initiating an activity or events. Examples include soliciting an answer to your question, unsolicited feedback, or a sentiment statement initiated by you. _____

Assistance from Others
Interaction that requires using others to assist you in any activity appropriate for the context that you request. Examples include learning, apprenticeship, and feedback. _____

Initiated Shared Activity
Interaction that involves doing things together with the group or a potential contact, but with you making the decision about "what to do." Examples include community initiatives, charitable causes, and organizing group events that you lead. _____

Incentives
Interaction that goes beyond participation and requires the giving of physical or tangible rewards to the group or potential contact. Examples include company swag, birthday gifts and cards, holiday gifts and cards, and cash. _____

Compliments
Interaction that involves giving praise or public acknowledgment to potential contacts or the group. Examples include positive feedback to others, encouraging words that express sentiment, another form of gratitude for sharing or giving, etc. _____

Impression Management
Interaction that focuses on managing appearance or actions in order to present a favorable symbolic image to others. Examples include storytelling of experiences and accomplishments, stating knowledge to signify expertise, association, and playing politics. _____

Direct Inquiry
Interaction that refers to directly seeking out a contact to talk about an issue or question. Examples include those topics focused on learning and self-improvement. _____

Bragging

Interaction focused on enhanced or embellished statements that are self-promoting in nature and are not used as humor. Examples include any of these types of conversations with the central character as yourself and how absolutely wonderful you are. _____

Sparking a Movement

Interaction that express your values by making a stand and working to get others to buy in to the cause. Examples include any type of conversation that supports an existing movement and for definition purposes does not include leading or starting a movement that you initiate. _____

Emotional Disclosure

Interaction that requires directly expressing feelings, likes, dislikes, etc., designed to expedite or get immediate results. Examples include nearly any type of intimate conversation as long as vulnerability is expressed and the emotional disclosure is not a form of bragging. _____

Self-Acceptance

Interaction where you demonstrate a comfortable acceptance of yourself, and express (directly or indirectly) that there is no need to change anything about you. Examples include nearly every conversation type and very similar to emotional disclosure except vulnerability is non-existent; meaning a form of self-actualization where any conversation is broached and literally nothing is considered off limits–total transparency. _____

Evaluating Your Score:

14-21: Too self conscious. Build relationships with anything scored higher than a 2 or 3. Once established, practice other lower scored tactics on contacts. Avoid the temptation of practicing with an anonymous profile.

22-45: Great range. Focus on activities you rated as 4's and 5's. It may make sense to learn to get comfortable with anything scored with a 3, especially if it is a preferred form of interaction in the network you are participating in.

46 and up: Open and willing. You are well positioned. Ensure you pace your level of intimacy with that of your environment. In a professional setting, avoid alienating yourself with too much intimacy.

Establishing and demonstrating your value is more than mere fact-finding. It is about interaction and conversation. The process of integration, as well as the relationships you build, ultimately give way to varying degrees of intimacy. This is the critical point where what you know and what you do converts into social capital.

e-Professionalism and Net Etiquette

It used to be, and probably still is, that good manners evolved from common sense. Now in most circumstances, business professionals are expected to understand etiquette. Granted, we are all interpreting to some degree the rules of etiquette within the ever-evolving technology paradigm. This, however, is not an excuse to ignore how your mannerisms reflect online.

Although the Internet is relatively a recent development, professional networking online has experienced rapid maturity. Many folks have adapted these concepts, but the ethics of what is appropriate has not been adapted quite so well; especially in subjective areas, like the use of emoticons, for instance.

As the speed of technology development accelerates, a professional in the virtual world must hold true to a few tenets: etiquette and knowledge of the pitfalls to avoid. This remains true until a universal guideline is created and broadly accepted.

Net Etiquette

These are the things that keep us grounded as new and dynamic tools for interaction continue to emerge. Techniques are good, but etiquette helps us frame our interaction online using fundamental tenets.

Keep these tenets in mind as you participate:

- **Participate and participate well.** It is better to not participate than to add no value. Do not post your company or any services or products you offer in a comment or post, unless someone requests it. This, to the Internet Culture as a whole, is considered SPAM, and it is highly undesirable.
- **Stay on topic and keep it short.** It is very easy to go off on a tangent. At the same time, you may have multiple points you want to discuss. Bear in mind, attention spans are getting shorter. Select the most important points to you and use only these. If making a comment, show respect and add value by staying on topic.
- **Avoid slamming someone in public.** Regardless if the comment or post you respond to is offensive, always give others the benefit of the doubt. Post your point of view, but do it professionally. Consider that there will always be topics you disagree with.

- **Follow up quickly to posts or comments directed at you.** Most people understand that there is lag online. Still try to give people some indication that you have received the message. If you don't have a response, it is ok to say, "Hey thanks, let me think about that and get back to you." It is viewed as courteous within the network to show that if someone is willing to add to your content, you will reciprocate with a response.
- **Be a linker.** If you have quoted someone, take the effort to give them credit by linking to them. Also, link to sources as a way to build credibility. Linking rich media like podcast and video is a great way to make anyone's content shine.

PROFESSIONAL SIGNAL ASSESSMENT

Your role, your years of experience, and what you may have to offer holds little value if your signals are not accurately conveyed. Keep in mind, your networking practices are viewed through a narrative lens, group acceptance and the co-production of meaning with group members.

Use the following four characteristics as a framework to vet and validate any signal you communicate:

1. **Character**–Build character with consistency. An aggressive, rebellious profile linked to mild and conservative profiles may be interpreted as a fictionalized performance, and others may question the circumstances that led to these anomalous connections. The network context can clarify ambiguous presentation, moderate an extreme performance, and confirm an ambitious one. *Hint:* Make sure your presence is accurate, succinct, and concise with little to no ambiguous statements.

2. **Trustworthiness**–Trusted weak ties are very useful sources of information and opportunities. Do your connections, the number of connections, and the age of connections show your trustworthiness? Remember, people trust new information and acquaintances that come to them via people they trust. If possible, have a contact or a tie mediate your signal. When people indiscriminately add connections, others who trusted their judgment suffer, and may eventually cease trusting them as a source for useful vouching. *Hint:* Use existing strong ties to build reliability and credibility to your activities.

3. **Relevance**–Are your activities relevant, or random and driven by emotion? Your relevancy is determined by how often you and your content are engaged, as demonstrated by feedback, number of ties, and exchange with others. *Hint:* Reserve developing professional content until you know people will add to your content and show you regard.

4. **Proven Experience**–Most relationships are characterized by the public activity between contacts. Ask yourself whether your interactions signal tie strength and subject-matter expertise. The same applies to content. The more work, research, activities (within reason) you are able to do online, the more likely your expertise is discovered and thus, the signal interpretation time is reduced. *Hint:* Develop weak ties to expand the scale of your network and scope of your work–an expression of your expertise through the influence and authority you carry.

Staying in Fashion

Signaling comes about as a result of your profile and any relational activity you engage in. There are a variety of signals sent and received within the social web and more specifically in a professional SBS, but for the sake of simplicity, I will focus on just one. It is known as fashion. And while the term implies the latest clothing styles, I will use it a bit differently.

Just as styles change each season and each year, fashions are signals that change frequently. In other words, fashion is about information, about being aware of the shifting social meaning of an object or method. Information fashions, when used appropriately, can create virtual invitations and allow those in the know to recognize others within their subculture via a common understanding of jokes, references, concepts, and phrases that have not yet spread to the mainstream.

Are you among the earliest adopters, willing to risk mistakes, spending months to learn a new computer language only to see it abandoned by its developers? Or among another group, knowing the choices you make have been vetted by numerous predecessors–safe, but not leading edge?

An example of this can be seen through the successful blog topics that follow the classic innovation diffusion model:

- You are a creative, but perhaps unknown, innovator who introduces a link.
- Highly connected "A-list" bloggers popularize it.
- It diffuses, over a period of weeks, through the rest of the population.
- This makes you an authority.

Staying in fashion is critical for success and maintaining vitality in your professional space.

Being or staying in fashion–whether via physical clothing or online linking–signals fitness in the continuously changing information world. It signals status in a society that values information prowess, the ability to distinguish between good and bad information, and the willingness to adapt to the changes brought by new information. This makes you influential.

The rewards of being a leader are status and influence. The costs are the energy it requires and the risk of mistaken judgment. Even in the world of blogs, where fashion is in the ostensible "free" medium of information, being at the forefront is costly. Time is required to find and disseminate new ideas, and publishing erroneous content is risky.

The secret is to avoid trying to stay in fashion with the tools and technology unless you have the time or resources to quickly ramp up. Although they will be important to incorporate as part of a broader adoption, staying in information fashion is much more productive. Best practices involve thoughts and concepts and these are much less likely to become a passing fad.

Becoming influential won't happen because you were the first to adopt Twitter or the next generation tool. True business professionals know it's not the tools that signal influence but by the type of information you convey and the manner in which you convey it.

We stay in fashion by knowing the right people and the right terms. Know the words, and the most talked about topics—and stay in fashion with time-tested trends and newly morphed insights. If something interesting emerges, lean towards discussing common topics with a twist, rather than the latest fad. You are not required to say and know the greatest next thing.

A trending tool like Google Trends or Yahoo! Buzz is very helpful to verify where a particular concept lies. These tools help determine which words are being actively used, and they provide you with insight into the current trends. The trend analysis exercise ought to be performed periodically and especially anytime you discover or uncover another buzzword or phrase that describes you or your industry.

Google Alerts is also helpful. Create at most three alerts relevant to a skill, industry, and competitor. The words used should be comprehensive, yet concise. You can always change your alerts later, or include more as you go along. You will realize the effectiveness of this tool, for all recent and hot topics, as you read the alerts you receive in your inbox each day or week. Remember also to vet them using a trend tool before you use them.

Classic Style in Information Fashion

The easiest way to get integrated with a network and engage others is to discuss common topics of the group. Researchers at Stanford University, in a study about popularity,[2] measured the relative celebrity of baseball players to demonstrate this theory. They chose this route over using movie stars or singers because they were able to objectively measure players' achievements on the field, making it possible to compare their level of stardom. One group of volunteers was provided a list of players and their statistics, and was asked to strike up an email conversation with a second group of volunteers. Two-thirds of the volunteers chose to discuss well-known players, even when they were long past their prime, but they ignored obscure players who put up great numbers the previous years. Even the more baseball-savvy participants gravitated toward the aging stars. These subject-savvy "experts" had the knowledge to inform the others about the rising stars, but instead chose to continue feeding participants the information they already knew. Researchers determined they behaved this way to establish a connection.

It's that hunger for connection, researchers say, that creates relationships and bonds. We innately know it will serve as social currency, and connect us to a larger conversation. Trying to come off as smart or too intelligent is condescending and puts people off.

Information fashion is not about the latest fads, but a classic style relative to your area of expertise. Essentially, common topics allow for bonding and connection, and people yearn for that. Start there and build relationships, then throw in your thoughts and show the talents of your knowledge; that's what it means to stay in fashion–information fashion, that is.

Engagement Tactics

In order to activate our personal networks we must be able to identify the flow of information, specifically those who create it and those who add value to it. In social business, knowing who influences information makes you resource-rich. To achieve any type of control, or even some sanity, in understanding the world you now live in, you must know who is influencing the information.

Evaluating Influence

Before committing to a regular activity and managing your reputation, you need to get deeply familiarized with the conversations in existing online networks. This context-awareness will help as you develop your own unique brand of e-professionalism.

The next step is to identify the leaders of these networks–those individuals who have influence over the audience based on their expertise, association, and commitment to the community. As you recall, most SBS have ratings, testimonials, and discussion features where you can easily discover who they are. These leaders, once identified, will be the targets of your outreach efforts, and the people with whom you will want to ingratiate yourself.

Influencers don't fit a standard profile but they have distinct appeal to their unique audiences. To identify the influencers, remember to stay true to your own profession and ask yourself these six questions:

- If they have a blog, what is the number of blog posts they have?
- How many inbound links do they have?
- How many followers do they have?
- What is the quality of their discussions?
- What do they know? Is it relevant to your industry?
- Whom are they acquainted with? Are their acquaintances peers or influencers?

Learning to become an influencer is as much of an effective strategy as it is to build a relationship with them. Take the time to study them and glean from them as much as you can. Do not worry too much about what you should be looking for, because as you are observing them, your unconscious mind is automatically picking up the tactics and mannerisms you will be comfortable with.

Science has demonstrated that humans are not beyond the old adage, "monkey see, monkey do." In 2009, researchers[3] found that imitation is part of our evolution. In fact, this imitation is a way of bonding, a social glue of sorts, because ultimately people are most comfortable with people like themselves. The same research also showed that the longer someone watches another, the more often the imitation is, and the more likely the imitation will become authentic.

This shouldn't be a shock. We imitate our heroes, our parents, our friends, and co-workers. The simple strategy is to surround yourself with winners or people with tenacity or, at a minimum, something you admire about them.

It is a challenge and much more difficult to hang out with people who tend to make you feel sometimes less valued. But keep in mind that you will eventually imitate–it is in your genetic code–and when you do, it will be for the better.

Influencers' Swagger

Consider this: influencers became influencers by finding and following other influencers. To be an influencer you must first understand the behaviors they exhibit. What makes them stand out? By identifying key behaviors of these online influencers, a research study conducted by MS&L[4] outlined the following program for maximizing digital influence:

1. **Understand other influencers' motivations:** High level of interest, sense of responsibility, joining the green movement, offline triggers (industry, association, and work memberships)
2. **Know where to find them:** search engines and portals, general news media sites, web sites of publications
3. **Understand what they share and the sources they gather from:** news media sites, web sites of publications, nonprofits, academic sites
4. **Create content that resonates:** green living, energy conservation, charities, local and global environmental issues
5. **Tailor content to their audience:** friends and family, colleagues, peers, members
6. **Tailor content to sharing methods:** verbal, e-mail, podcasts, comments, etc.

BEST PRACTICE REVIEW

These days there are many ways to reach and impact people's lives online. You can upload professional or even personal photos to reach people, you could Tweet and provide mini-status updates to get information to people quickly, you can exchange links and articles on Del.icio.us and Digg, respectively. The possibilities are endless.

You may use any tool within what is accepted in your professional environment to build your online reputation, but tools and technology fade quickly. Thus, the best practices[5] presented here are for the following four (4) tools proven through real-world cases to be fundamental to any social business professional.

Blogs:

Use: State an opinion, describe a solution, point to something interesting, ponder an idea or broadcast some message

Shape: Top-heavy, with a longer initial message, similar to a magazine article, however, it is perfectly fine to have a small number of comments

Language: Informal or formal and in the first person

Unlike discussions or documents, blogs are openly visible and normally not restricted as part of an online community or network. When trying to broadcast a particular message, this is the best forum to use. Blogs also capture and maintain valuable knowledge and thought processes for your particular expertise or domain. By sharing your thoughts, you maximize your influence and demonstrate knowledge and passion in your field.

Discussion/Forums:

Use: Get feedback, report a problem, find a solution to a problem

Shape: Bottom-heavy, with a shorter initial message and a large number of replies and comments

Language: Informal and in the first person

Use a discussion as a forum to ask questions and get answers. Discussions enable you to overcome the handicap inherent in static knowledge resources or when search results reach a dead end. Since discussions support multiple, or branched, threads, it is an easy way to get included into a conversation.

Considered one of the first social media tools, you can find a discussion nearly anywhere online.

Wiki or Online Documents:

Use: Codify existing knowledge, document processes, create a report, best practices, and meeting notes

Shape: Topy heavy with a longer initial message

Language: Formal and in the third person

Without a doubt, today's most popular collaborative document tool, or wiki, is Wikipedia. A wiki is a type of website that allows the visitors to easily add, remove, and otherwise edit content (as wiki syntax is being slowly eliminated, online documents are emerging as the replacement. Many of the user principles are the same. A couple examples of publicly available online documents are MS Office online and Google Documents). In addition to content such as text, wiki entries often include links to related articles, blog entries, and references. Because wikis support multiple authors and editors, they are a great way to co-produce with others in your industry and quickly integrate yourself into a group.

Social Networking:

Use: To meet and manage new contacts

Shape: IM, widgets, events, profiles, etc.

Language: Other

This category gets broader everyday, but its fundamental use is to meet others. Social networks created by social networking is a key to building reliability and credibility in your field or area of expertise. Use with caution, as traditional social networks have many professional or career-ending traps associated with them. Stay within professional networks, if possible, and use these sparingly along with presence-building activities. Pick up only the tools that are recommended to you, so that you can also adopt any lessons learned from the recommender.

Greatest Secret Weapon

After identifying and evaluating the influencers, it is time to start engaging with them on a deeper level. Gift giving is one way to do this.

Gift giving is an art, but once mastered one of the most effective tools in your toolkit for engagement. Gift giving for our purposes means gifts of information and contacts, and as simple as it may seem, it comes in many forms. Famed Peter Drucker in New Realities[6] offers this perspective: "Information that changes something or somebody– either by becoming grounds for action, or by making an individual (or institution) capable of different or more effective action."

These gifts are easy to identify; they come with no noticeable motive and they give the receiver something of value or something they desire. There are countless stories of software programmers and web developers scouring the Internet for information about a particular technical issue that wasn't solved until someone gave them the answer. This answer, quite often, was something obscure but took only a fraction of the time to resolve by someone with the knowledge and expertise.

The act of giving a gift turns information into knowledge and the gift reciprocated is knowledge that has already been codified, and sometimes wisdom that could have otherwise taken exponentially longer to acquire yourself.

Gifting allows you to navigate large information spaces. When you gift and others gift back, you get two things: 1) a reciprocal relationship that you know and can soon rely on, and 2) you get to very quickly quantify and aggregate information vetted by others.

Power of Gifting

According to Colin Camerer,[7] a professor at the University of Pennsylvania, a formal game-theoretic model showed us that gifts serve as "signals" of a person's intentions about future investments in a relationship. Inefficient gifts, says Camerer, can be a better signal. His research shows us that giving gifts, like a kind word or a supportive comment, have an underlying cultural meaning that allow us to build relationships with each other easier and faster than giving an efficient gift like cash.

Camerer's experiment begins with two players who are either co-workers or prospective business partners. They will separately choose whether or not to invest within a fixed period of time. The model requires that the investment (gift) be without restriction and therefore no contract can be defined. This keeps the central element (regard) as an unknown variable: will your other partner invest or reciprocate?

The gifting experiment found that players will not invest early in a relationship when the probability of reciprocation is low or the cost of non-compliance (rejection or reputation damage) is abnormally large. Players did invest if they could somehow discover a partner's motivations, and if those motivations were aligned with his own. If you are willingly giving to the group (for example, you go through the trials of assimilation or steps to full membership), although they do not know you, they will invest or reciprocate.

The major finding was that the other player needed some indicator or signal that was too costly to fake. Enter the information gift, where the cost is time and the value is information. Thus, you can not lose when gifting is performed correctly for two reasons: *precedence* and *obligation*.

The implication here is that the gifts, even when they fail, give way to a deeper meaning for the original gift giver. Basically, if you are a member, a willing investor in relationships, and thoughtful enough to deliver a gift to someone with a good probability that they would reciprocate, even if they don't reciprocate your gift, there are far-reaching implications within a network or community. Beyond breaking of the social norm, it leaves a *precedence* of the receiver. This precedence may or may not actually affect reputation, but it creates the perception that it does.

Peter Blau, Columbia University Sociology Professor,[8] posited that status is an emergent property of social exchange: A person who gives others valuable gifts or bestows important services makes a claim for superior status by obliging the receivers to him. If the receivers return benefits that adequately discharge their obligation, they deny the giver his claim to superiority. This is the reason why many people do not like accepting gifts from people they do not know.

Blau constructed his theory of exchange and status on the basis of his observations of behavioral patterns of employees in a law enforcement agency. He noted that workers who lacked expertise to perform a task behaved deferentially towards others who had more knowledge, in hope that the skilled workers would share their know-how. In other words, technical knowledge and deference were exchanged between employees. Blau argued that individuals use their know-how to give others advice as a gift so as to gain status. Status, expressed through deference, was returned, and thus created a working relationship. This means that group members are likely to reciprocate in order to alleviate any *obligation*, or relinquishing of power they perceive to have within the group.

Stages of Me Paradox Success

Networks are now a global metropolis, vast and heterogeneous, and in this environment individuals and groups need many things One example is protection from being hijacked by anything from pop-up ads to SPAM and online scams. There are numerous others that we have explored, but ultimately, it is the development of relationships that makes it all possible, especially the Me Paradox.

Relationships are so fundamental that often we overlook the system that makes it so. Like any system, there are inputs and outputs, but the mechanism that keeps it all together is reliance. Reputations are built on consistency. But its corollary, reliability, is what builds relationships.

Reliance is built over three (3) stages that take you from someone unknown into a weak or strong tie whom others exchange with. Understand the dynamics of these phases and then incorporate gift giving as a means to navigate through each phase.

Stage 1: Competence

You are unknown. You just joined a network and only have a few pieces of content, an online profile, perhaps, and a loosely relatable reputation resulting from a search. The goal at this stage is to leave an impression, a professional signal that matches who you are and what you represent with your actions and style. This should be a consistent signal, and one that leaves an impression of competence.

In Stage 1, rather than grabbing attention by any means, build relationships with others that are able to vouch for you by showing your willingness to invest in the group. Recall the *Warranting Principle*, which reminds us that people tend to believe what is said as long as they get the impression that the person is not directly influenced or experiencing gains from having said it. Basically, the strategy involves letting others say it to make it much more believable. Use a form of gift giving, but don't be too intimate. For instance, offering someone unsolicited advice to a recent issue, although intended for learning purposes, is an initiation activity that may be too personal, and it also may create a sense of obligation for someone with, say, a higher status. Since you are unfamiliar to them, they may mistake the activity as bragging or create an obligation they are uncomfortable with, and therefore openly refuse your gift. Recognize the type of content it is, and then add value by providing positive feedback–something that has a low intimacy level. You wouldn't give a woman a diamond ring on your first date would you?

We use gift giving to get us contacts and build relationships. Giving gifts is something that is done when you are able to provide information or contacts that sit at the relative left end in our *Wheel of Conversations* (see figure 9-1). For instance, giving positive feedback on a member's post or responding to a photo a member has uploaded with a comment that signals a positive sentiment–that is a simple yet effective gift.

Don't worry if they do not reciprocate; the record of the gift will exist as you advance onto the next stage. In addition, if they do not gift back, consider it as an indication that you've reached someone in a much higher status (even if only perceived). Pull back and select someone with a lesser status.

The secret is to build enough social capital through gift giving that when you create content, you can get someone credible to reply or reciprocate. This then becomes an opportunity to share in someone's credibility; avoid any initiation activities (for example, creating content, asking for an introduction, or testimonial) until your gifts are regularly reciprocated, which signals that your competence has been established and you may now move onto the next stage.

Stage 2: Predictability

The association with great experiences must be tied to your reputation. Don't make the mistake of using social capital like a credit card, where you are in huge amount of debt and other creditors are reluctant to extend you credit. Consider, instead, the Me Paradox. Who you are is a composite of people's experiences, especially online. The repeated and concerted effort to maintain a specific reputation is the way to further your successes.

For professionals, a good attitude and a signal of competence is the most you can ask for at this stage. Do not strive for too much and dilute your brand. Stick to the activities you are known for, the ones people can rely on. The investment is too great to develop multiple streams of competencies, so don't try to be everything to everyone.

At this stage, you should continue gifting and even at more intimate levels. The gifting will continue to create an information and relationship exchange, which quickly gives way, like no other process or technology out there, to a faster more efficient way to build your own reputation. As such, the use of gifting as a vehicle for regard ensures the attention is authentic, personalized, and transparent.

Any suspicion of hidden agendas will lead to mistrust, and eventually a damaged reputation. Gifting, when performed correctly, not only builds reputation, but also acknowledgment, acceptance, respect, status, power, intimacy, love, friendship, kinship, and sociability, to name only a few.

Most importantly in this stage, you need to be predictable; even if it is for something that does not exemplify your core skill or strength. The continual push of communication, content, link density, and testimonials builds trust in the experience one can expect as they engage with you. As trust is established, even for those who never interacted with you before, you are able to develop additional streams of intimacies and relation activities, which lead to the establishment of quicker and tighter bonds, hence strong predictability.

Stage 3: Cognitive and Emotional Dependability

With competence and predictability, people will want to engage with you. They want to be your friend, have you help them, or procure your services–this is where their expectations are matched with the experience. When you nail signal accuracy, cognitive and emotional dependability is inevitable. At Stage 3, this matching of expectation with experience requires you to know their expectations. It might be as simple as searching or soliciting feedback about what others have thought about their interaction with you–candidly. This is an iterative process, where you continually work to not necessary improve, but to adjust to meet the expectations with the experience. Signal alignment, as long as it is founded on competence and predictability, is how you are able to win their feelings of attachment.

Cognitive and emotional dependability is the point of support and sanction, where even if damaging or negative commentary were spread about you, the tie will be reluctant to accept it and will often defend you. They will have high sentiment towards you. The only disadvantage here is that the stronger the attachment and the stronger the emotions involved, the more likely you will be perceived as a greater threat to others within this power struggle. Ensure that you are good to your loyal advocates; remember that they are your support infrastructure–once you get them to this stage, even as a latent tie, you can utilize them when you need to.

Recap

All our lives we integrate into groups, schools, churches, and jobs; the only difference now is the medium. By understanding the tactics and behaviors of a social business professional, it keeps you focused, economizes your time and effort, and if you have learned anything, keeps you consistent in your efforts and activities.

The Me Paradox works best when you rely on people within your personal network. Connections without regard, thousands of random connections on a social network, typically do not fall within the realm of the paradox. By working smart and using the engagement strategies, you will be able to identify with those ever-so-important information mediators–those with social capital. Your success is sure to follow.

~chapter ten~
Final Thoughts

$\mathbb{C}$ompanies are changing and soon they will be searching for people-centric prospects who are facilitators of solving people's problems–natural gift givers.

Paul Greenberg,[1] famed CRM guru, once built a company in the '80s by going to Usenets and scouring through every thread of IBM Lotus software discussions. When he identified a natural gift giver, he recruited him. Basically, he searched for those who helped someone and when there was a response with a 'thank you; that helped' attached to the thread, he knew he had found a natural gift giver with subject-matter expertise. He recruited 65 Lotus developers this way and eventually became the number one authorized Lotus partner for IBM, out of some 17,000 registered partners.

As seen in Yahoo!,[2] the Pope, whose own web presence has escalated, recently urged priests to use all multimedia tools at their disposal to preach the Gospel and engage in dialogue with people of other religions and cultures. As natural gift givers already, priests were encouraged to use cutting-edge technologies to express themselves and lead their communities. In a message released by the Vatican titled, *The Priest and Pastoral Ministry in a Digital World: New Media at the Service of the Word*, Pope Benedict urged priests to use special care when initiating contact with other cultures. The message was aimed at encouraging reflection in the church on the positive uses of new media.

The Pope believes in using new media to give the gift of religion. If we put the same faith in these unselfish tactics, as does the Catholic Church, we can gain a strategic advantage in our professional lives.

Online Reputation Management
Step 1: You build a profile
Step 2: You find a network
Step 3: You engage
…And then **repeat**!

To recap what we have learned about the lifecycle, let's go back to the priests as an example, so we can examine how it all comes together.

As the priests think about their online presence, they consider their goals, and find appropriate keywords to match. Then, as they develop their general online profile, they carefully choose keywords for each distinct profile field, and strategic placements to reach high ranking in search engine results or in their Google Quotient, for say "Roman Catholic Priests." It is easy to see how this can apply to your own goals.

Next, like the priests, you will find the appropriate network for what you want to achieve. Capture how the audience and your activities align to meet your goals. If it is converting the next generation of Catholics, then selecting a music-centric network may not work, but a theology network or a network where people are looking for spiritual guidance might be ideal. If you are looking to broadcast your message, then having your own network—for example a blog or web presence—is a good strategy; keep in mind, you do not necessarily need to do everything within an existing network. By evaluating other blogs and blog rolls as linkages to your content and your web presence, you are, in essence, creating your own network.

Although gift giving is the core activity, engagement cannot begin with giving gifts. The starting point is the role we play, who we decide we will be within a network. Select a role that best aligns with your goals and who you are. The number one mistake is trying to be everything to everyone; focus on finding your voice, how you fit in according to the audience you engage with. This means, in order to send authentic signals, you need an honest evaluation of your comfort level in terms of intimacy and an understanding of how that complements the relational activities of the audience. What types of interactions are we comfortable with? What type of interactions do the members of the network prefer? How is social capital generated there?

Within any non-religious network, the priests from our example may need to take on a role of friend rather than spiritual advisor. Otherwise, any attempts at gift giving may be seen as a deceptive sales tactic. There may, in fact, be some members who are looking for spiritual guidance, and the priests are equipped to offer that gift of spirituality. However, if the priests don't take into account the relational activities members are comfortable with, they will find their signals are ill-received.

When you give gifts they must be without explicit intent, in other words, inefficient. We are not talking about the free T-shirt as long as you apply for a credit card gimmick—we all know this is a trap, a persuasion tactic. You as a member, a person with great integrity and a giving heart, want to help people (perception of altruism); and you naturally expect people to reciprocate (intention of mutualism). You are willing to be the first to give—the first to initiate the effort of membership, group forming, networking, and friendship. The members wanting and needing spiritual guidance may only accept this type of interaction when meaningful signals identify you as a friend who can be trusted, not a clergyman.

Interaction according to the network is about identity and relations. Your story, which includes your profile and the way you engage within the network, should accurately reflect the signals you communicate. The continuous effort of signal alignment is the cornerstone of any successful engagement strategy.

The Full Lifecycle

The Paradox of Me is about interconnection and interdependence. As the methods for this improve, we can start to see how one single action has infinite ramifications. Do not fall for the immediacy of the tools and technology available on the Internet. Results take time to germinate. Once rooted though, online reputation and relationships will become your most vital resource so do not take short cuts, and do not throw all your efforts away on a whim or an impulsive emotion. Although short-run opportunities are abound and many stories are told to this fact, you must use the lag as an advantage and consider what works in the long run. Short-term actions that result in short-term gains are more than likely reputation killers. The online reputation lifecycle will let you know when it is time to repeat. Enter each phase with care and nurture it like any other delicate resource. Because of the obviousness in which the digital world operates, the time for the lifecycle to repeat will present itself as robust results–something with legs that stands on its own.

Glossary

Blogosphere is made up of all blogs and their inter-connections.

Blogroll. A blogroll is a list of links to blogs that the blogger likes. A blogroll is usually included in the blog's sidebar.

Coalition. According to Douglas H. Yarn who wrote *The Dictionary of Conflict Resolution* in 1991, a coalition is a temporary alliance or partnering of groups in order to achieve a common purpose or to engage in joint activity and coalition building is the process by which parties come together to form a coalition.

Collective Intelligence is a shared or group intelligence that emerges from the collaboration and competition of many individuals and appears in consensus decision making in computer networks.

Enterprise 2.0. Andrew P. McAfee, assistant professor at the Harvard Business School who is said to have proposed the term of 'Enterprise 2.0' for the first time, defines it as the use of emergent social software platforms within companies, or between companies and their partners or customers.

Fakester. First used by a Friendster user and popularized by Danah Boyd, Fakesters are people who join social networks and put up fake personas.

Folksonomy. Thomas Vander Wal, an information architect and Internet developer, has dubbed folksonomy-a people's taxonomy-the new approach to categorization on the Internet.

Geotagging. This is the process of adding geographical identification metadata to various media such as photographs, video, websites, or RSS feeds. It can help users find a wide variety of location-specific information. For instance, one can find images taken such as geotagging-enabled information services that can potentially be used to find location-based news, websites, or other resources.

Long Tail. Often presented as a phenomenon of interest primarily to mass market retailers and web-based businesses, the Long Tail also has implications for the producers of content online. The Long Tail describes a niche strategy of producing large quantities by the accumulation of many unique items of small quantities.

Millennials. Also called **Generation Y**, it is roughly defined by people with birthdates between 1979 and 2000. They are characterized as the generation who does not remember a world without computers and mobile phones. They do not fear self expression and have strong opinions, especially towards bureaucracy.

Network Effect. Network effects become significant after a certain subscription percentage has been achieved, called critical mass. At the critical mass point, the value obtained from the good or service is greater than or equal to the price paid for the good or service

New Economy. On harvardbusiness.org, Umair Haque in his *2009 Smart Growth Manifesto*, discusses four pillars of the New Economy: 1) Outcomes, not incomes, 2) Connections, not transactions, 3) People, not products, and 4) Creativity, not productivity.

Social Business is the term used to describe this profound reshaping of the global business landscape. It allows and rewards open conversation between colleagues, partners and customers, and relies on the power of social connections to shape new products and services.

SPLOGS is SPAM in the form of a blog. Normally these are automated postings that duplicate content in order to artificially increase search engine ranking.

Tacit Knowledge is knowledge that is difficult to transfer to another person by means of writing it down or verbalizing it.

Warranting Principle. It posits that perceivers' judgments about a target rely more heavily on information which the targets themselves cannot manipulate, than on self-descriptions.

Web 2.0. Web 2.0 technologies include wikis, blogs, RSS, online social networks, virtual communities, social network analysis, social bookmarking, social tagging, web services, AJAX, JSON, and podcasting.

End Notes

Chapter 1:

1. OnOrbit.com – NASA Generation Y Perspectives 2008 by Keith Cowing
2. According to Lowell Bryan, Eric Matson, and Leigh Weiss' report Harnessing the power of informal employee networks.
3. Gartner Inc., a leading information technology research and consulting company, estimates that the frequency of non-routine situations requiring tacit knowledge (collaborating, exchanging information, making judgments, and drawing on knowledge from coworkers, customers, and suppliers to make decisions) will double between 2006 and 2010.
4. According to Jive, Social Business is the new "business architecture" and the new community is the "social capital marketplace" where intellectual capital is coupled with relationships.
5. Levine, R., Locke, C., Searls, D., Weinberger, D. (2001). *The Cluetrain Manifesto: The End of Business as Usual*. Cambridge: Basic Books,
6. 2007 O'Reilly Radar – *Web 2.0 Principles and Best Practices* by John Musser with Tim O'Reilly and the Radar Team.
7. Pew Internet & American Life Project 2006 – Home Broadband Adoption by John B. Horrigan.
8. GSMA represents the interests of the worldwide mobile communications industry.
9. Facebook' Press Room Q4 2009
10. Technorati's State of the Blogosphere 2008 report
11. Google's Fourth Quarter and Fiscal Year 2009 Results
12. Pew Internet & American Life Project 2007 – Project Data Memo by Amanda Lenhart and Mary Madden.
13. See #6
14. The 2.0 Adoption Council – The State of Enterprise 2.0 Adoption Q4 2009. Council members work in large enterprises where 76% represent organizations larger than 10,000 employees. These stats are not that of small start-ups experimenting with new

technologies, but rather the embracing of technology by major, established global enterprises.

15. According to Oliver Young's *Global Enterprise Web 2.0 Market Forecast: 2007 To 2013*
16. In December 2008 both Lycos and Google released their list of the top searched terms for 2008.
17. For more information read *The Wisdom of Crowds: Why the Many Are Smarter Than the Few and How Collective Wisdom Shapes Business, Economies, Societies and Nations*, published in 2004, written by James Surowiecki.

Chapter 2:

1. See Chapter 1 Notes # 2
2. Reed, D. (Feb. 2001). The law of the pack. *Harvard Business Review*, 2--3.
3. April 20, 2009, CBC News article 'Candidate's racy Facebook photos showed 'lack of judgment': B.C. NDP leader'
4. Garton, L., C. Haythornthwaite and B. Wellman (1997) 'Studying Online Social Networks', *Journal of Computer-Mediated Communication 3*(1).
5. Liu, H. (2007). Social network profiles as taste performances. *Journal of Computer-Mediated Communication, 13*(1), article 13.
6. Weitzner, D. (2007). Beyond Secrecy – New Privacy Protection Strategies for Open Information Spaces. *IEEE Internet Computing, Technology & Society*
7. Solove, D. (2007). *The future of reputation: Gossip, rumor, and privacy on the Internet*. New Haven: Yale University Press.
8. The 2009 study conducted by Harris Interactive for CareerBuilder.com that questioned 2,667 managers and human resource workers revealed that prospective employers use social networks more than ever to check out job applicants.
9. Laney, M.O. (2002). *The introvert advantage: How to thrive in an extrovert world*. New York: Workman.
10. Jones, D. (2006). Not all successful CEOs are extroverts. *USA Today*, 7 June.
11. See #9

12. Fombrun, C., Gardberg, N. and Barnett, M. (2000). Opportunity platforms and safety nets: Corporate citizenship and reputational risk. *Business and Society Review, 105*, (1), pp. 85–106.

Chapter 3:

1. Intel OpenPort is one of a Jive's first SBS community. Intel OpenPort launched in 2007 and can be found at: communities dot intel dot com.
2. Walther, J. B., & Parks, M. R. (2002). *Cues filtered out, cues filtered in: Computer-mediated communication and relationships.* Thousand Oaks, CA: Sage.
3. There are many terrific books and resources out there, so reference them as needed and since this is not an SEO book, the goal is to only expose you to the tools, get you base-lined (have the basics, a plan and a go-forward strategy) and then arm you with skills necessary to be successful without going into the full background of SEO.
4. See (Brin, S., & Page, L. 1998. Anatomy of a large-scale hypertextual web search engine. In *Proceedings of the 7th International World Wide Web Conference* (Brisbane, Australia, Apr. 14 –18). pp. 107–117.) for more about Google's PageRank Algorithm

Chapter 4:

1. March 11, 2009 Forrester Report *US Telecommuting Forecast, 2009 to 2016* by Ted Schadler for Information & Knowledge Management Professionals.
2. The Gig Generation - The rise in what experts called "necessity entrepreneurship" is a normal consequence of a weak economy, also called the Gig Economy. Although it is accentuated in members of a Millennial Generation already inclined to be itinerant dabblers rather than lifelong cubicle fixtures, many more seemingly regular folks are working gigs these days.

Chapter 5:

1. Ding, Y., Gao, Q., & Rau, P. (2008). Relationships between the level of intimacy and lurking in online social network services. *Computers in Human Behavior, 24*, 2757-2770.
2. Seely-Brown, J. & Duguid, P. (2000). *The social life of information*. Boston: Harvard Business School Press.
3. *Connections. New Ways of Working in the Networked Organization* by Lee Sproull and Sara Kiesler (MIT Press, Cambridge, Mass., 1991).
4. Boyd, D. & Ellison, N. (2007). Social Network Sites: Definition, History and Scholarship. *Journal of Computer-Mediated Communication, 13*(1), article 1.
5. Social business software and social business sites are ostensibly the same, represented by the acronym SBS, used interchangeably. Social business software is the transportable platform that when used externally or made available online as a destination refers to social business [web]sites.
6. Spraggins, J. D. 2003. Review of "Cyberculture: Electronic mediation volume 4" by Pierre Levy. Minneapolis: University of Minnesota Press, 2001. *Soc. Sci. Comput. Rev. 2*(4) (Dec. 2003), 514-516.

Chapter 6:

1. aSmallWorld (asmallworld dot net) is a private community of internationally minded people from around the world.
2. SelectMinds' 2008 Research-based White Paper called *Corporate Social Networking: Increasing the density of connections to power business performance*
3. December 5, 2006 Report called *Predicts 2007: Big Changes Ahead in the High-Performance Workplace* written by T. Austin, D. Cearley, J. Mann, G. Phifer, D. Sholler, K. Harris, T. Bell, R. Knox, M. Cain, and M. Silver
4. See Chapter 1 Notes #6?
5. Sample List from Jive Software (Note not all networks are active or still using the same URL):

Developer SBS:
Palm: pdnet.palm.com/wps/portal/pdnet/developers
National Instruments: decibel.ni.com/content/community/zone
Cognos: communities.cognos.com/home
Webapplica: www.webapplica.org/clearspacex
Netezza: www.netezzacommunity.com
Curl: developers.curl.com
Tibco: www.tibcommunity.com
Progress: www.psdn.com/
Amazon: aws.amazon.com/connect
IBM: www-128.ibm.com/developerworks/community/
Oracle: forums.oracle.com/forums/
Sun: forum.java.sun.com/
Java Lobby: www.javalobby.org/
Citrix: support.citrix.com/forums/
RIM: www.blackberry.com/developers/community/index.shtml
Webwork OpenSymphony: forums.opensymphony.com
Hewlett-Packard: devresource.hp.com/forums
SAP: www.sdn.sap.com/irj/sdn/collaboration
Sony: developer.sonyericsson.com/index.jspa?categoryID=1
Symbian: developer.symbian.com/forum
Typo3: support.typo3.org:8080/jive
BEA: forums.bea.com/bea
Wipro: sparcs.wiprosupport.com:8080/seamlesstomorrow

Event/User Group SBS:
RSA (division of EMC): www.rsaconference.com
VMWorld: www.vmworld.com/vmworld/index.jspa?view=all
America's SAP User Group: www.asug.com/

Advocacy/Loyalty SBS:
Cisco: cisco.hosted.jivesoftware.com/index.jspa?ciscoHome=true
PC World: forums.pcworld.com
Informatica: my-prod.informatica.com/
Mac World: forums.macworld.com
NetApp: communities.netapp.com
SAP Plexus: plexus.sap.com
RedHat: rhx.redhat.com/rhx/catalog/products.jspa
eBay: community.worldofgood.com/index.jspa?
utm_campaign=oldsite&utm_medium=links&utm_source=worldofgood

Innovation SBS:
Sprint (Xohm): trials.xohm.com/
NetApp: communities.netapp.com
VMWare: communities.vmware.com

Partner SBS:
Brocade: www.brocade.com/partners/AlliancePartnerNetwork.jsp
Intel: communities.intel.com

Support SBS:
Good Technology (Motorola): www.good.com/begood/
Mentor Graphics: communities.mentor.com/mgcx
LANDesk Software: community.landesk.com/support/index.jspa?
showFeatureTour=false
Canon USA: www.support.cusa.canon.com/e2/shared/login.jsp
Convio: community.customer.convio.com/
Lotus Symphony: symphony.lotus.com/software/lotus/symphony/home.jspa
Borland: support.borland.com/kbindex.jspa
Bladelogic: www.bladelogic.com/supportRedirect.jsp
Tibco: www.tibco.com/services/support/supportweb.jsp
Veritas: communities.vmware.com
Citrix: support.citrix.com/
Icesoft: support.icesoft.com/jive
Autodesk: discussion.autodesk.com
Digital Advisor: www.digitaladvisor.com/digital-cameras/
Documentum: support.documentum.com/login/login.htm
Apple: discussions.apple.com
IONA (KB): www.iona.com/support/kb
Progress: www.progress.com/support/index.ssp
Toshiba: forums.computers.toshiba-europe.com
Checkpoint: forums.checkpoint.com/forums
Hyperic: forums.hyperic.com/jiveforums
Simple Devices: www.simplecenter.com/index.html
TeamDev: support.teamdev.com/category.jspa?categoryID=2

6. Dassault Systèmes SolidWorks is a 3D modeling software provider formed in 1993. Headquartered in Massachusetts, they support over one million designers around the world.
7. Bioinformatics' 2007 Survey called *The New Collaboration: Social Media and the Life Science Opportunity*
8. According to Jeffrey Mann's report Four Lessons Enterprises Can Learn from *Consumer Social Software* published February 1, 2008

Chapter 7:

1. Offer, A. (1997). Between the Gift and the Market: The Economy of Regard. *Economic History Review, 50* (3), 450-76.

2. Announced on April 21, 2010 at Facebook's F8 Developer Conference in San Francisco by Facebook Founder and CEO Mark Zuckerberg
3. Cialdini, R.B. (1993). *Influence: The psychology of persuasion* (Revised edition). New York: Quill.
4. Watkins, M. (2003). *The first 90 days: Critical success strategies for new leaders at all levels*. Boston: Harvard Business School Press.
5. Sebenius, J. & Lax, D. (1992). *Thinking Coalitionally: Party Arithmetic, Process Opportunism, and Strategic Sequencing*. In Negotiation Analysis, edited by H. Peyton Young. Ann Arbor: University of Michigan Press.
6. NWO (Netherlands Organization for Scientific Research) (2009, May). Half Of Your Friends Lost In Seven Years, Social Network Study Finds. *ScienceDaily*.
7. McPherson, M., Smith-Lovin, L., & Cook, J. (2001). Birds of a feather: Homophily in Social Networks. *Annual Review of Sociology, 27*, 415-444.
8. Klapwijk, A. & Van Lange, P. (2009). Promoting Cooperation and Trust in "Noisy" Situations: The Power of Generosity. *Journal of Personality and Social Psychology, 96* (1), 83–103
9. Nahapiet, J., & Ghoshal, S. (1998). Social capital, intellectual capital, and the organizational advantage. *The Academy of Management Review, 23*, 242–266.
10. Teten, D. & Allen, S. (2005). *The Virtual Handshake. Opening Doors and Closing Deals Online*. New York: AMACOM.

Chapter 8:

1. Quote from a Wikipedia article on Social Capital
2. Donath, J. ((2007). Signals in social supernets. *Journal of Computer-Mediated Communication*, 13(1), article 12.
3. On September 18, 2007, Dennis Ross spoke with Forbes.com about the "12 steps for effective negotiation"
4. DiMicco, J. & Millen, D. (2008). *People Sensemaking with Social Networking Sites*. Cambridge: IBM Research Lab,
5. Wikipedia's explanation of Gladwell's 2005 book *Blink*. "It presents in popular science format research from psychology and

behavioral economics on the adaptive unconscious; mental processes that work rapidly and automatically from relatively little information. It considers both the strengths of the adaptive unconscious, for example in expert judgment, and its pitfalls such as stereotypes."

6. Lifescience Staff article *Quick decisions might be the best* published on January 9, 2007
7. A 2008 LifeScience report says when it comes to making life-changing decisions, neither snap judgments nor "sleeping on it" trump good old-fashioned conscious thought. The finding supports a 2006 report made by Dutch researchers and published in the Journal of Science.
8. According to *New York Times* articles on July 17, 2007 and October 17, 2008, the Obama and McCain Campaigns reports current donations and spending statistics.
9. Hamel, G (2007). *The Future of Management*. Boston: Harvard Business Press.

Chapter 9:

1. Read more about Sean O'Driscoll at communitygrouptherapy dot com
2. According to Alice LaPlante's article *Seeking Common Ground in Conversations Can Stifle Innovation and Reward the Wrong People* published June 2009
3. According to Time Magazine Online writer John Cloud's August 17, 2009 article *Monkey See, Monkey Do: Why We Flatter Via Imitation*
4. By identifying key behaviors of online influencers, a research study conducted by MS&L outlined the following program for maximizing digital influence:
5. Adapted from best practices developed by Jive Software
6. Cheal, D. (1996). *Gifts in contemporary North America*. Bowling Green: Bowling Green State University Popular Press.
7. Camerer, C. (1988). Gifts as Economic Signals and Social Symbols. *Journal of Sociology, 94*, S180-S214.
8. Blau, P. (1998). *Exchange and Power in Social Life*. New Brunswick, NJ: Transaction.

Chapter 10:

1. Paul is considered a thought leader in CRM, having been published in numerous industry and business publications over the years. He is a member of the Destination CRM Board of Experts and the SearchCRM Expert Advisory Panel as well as a member of the Board of Advisors for GreaterChinaCRM for many years among many others.
2. Found on Yahoo! News Mashable, AP Ariel David's article *Pope to Priests: We Must Blog Now* on January 25, 2010

Index

www.ingramcontent.com/pod-product-compliance
Lightning Source LLC
Chambersburg PA
CBHW051229050326
40689CB00007B/855